TROLLEYS, TRAMS, AND LIGHT RAIL
AROUND THE WORLD

At Castle Shannon loop on May 18, 1983, Port Authority Transit (PAT) Presidents' Conference Committee (PCC) car No. 1713 is awaiting departure time for its northbound trip to downtown Pittsburgh, Pennsylvania. This was one of seventy-five PCC cars (Nos. 1700–1774) built by St. Louis Car Company and delivered to Pittsburgh Railways Company during December 1947 to May 1978. PAT painted numerous trolley cars in a variety of eye-catching paint schemes designed to enhance the image of public transit which actually increased transit ridership. (*Photographer Carl H. Sturner Used with permission from Audio Visual Designs [www.audiovisualdesigns.com]*)

On February 24, 1981, Companhia Carris de Ferro de Lisboa Route 22 tram No. 246 is passing Route 20 tram No. 740 in Lisbon, Portugal. Both of these trams were built by J.G. Brill Company in Philadelphia. (*Kenneth C. Springirth photograph*)

TROLLEYS, TRAMS, AND LIGHT RAIL

AROUND THE WORLD

Kenneth C. Springirth

FONTHILL

Basler Verkehrs-Betriebe (Basel Transport Service) (BVB) Route 3 car No. 446 (built by Schindler Wagon AG, Prattein) is in Basel Switzerland eastbound for Birsfelden Hard. In 2017, this line was extended into St. Louis France. BVB also has Route 8 which serves the neighboring German city of Weil am Rhein. This is the only tram system in the world that serves three different countries—Switzerland, France, and Germany. Hence it is possible to ride a Route 3 tram from France into Switzerland and transfer to a Route 8 tram to enter Germany. (*Kenneth C. Springirth photograph*)

On top portion of cover: On May 24, 1977, Melbourne & Metropolitan Tramways Board (MMTB) tram No. 258 is at Elizabeth and Flinders Street with the Flinders Street Station in the background in downtown Melbourne, Australia, awaiting departure time. This was one of 200 W2 class trams (numbered 219–418) that were introduced during 1927–1931. While some of these cars were withdrawn in the mid-1960s, others were withdrawn in 1977–1987. (*Kenneth C. Springirth photograph*)

On bottom portion of cover: Blackpool Tramway No. 59 known as "Dreadnought" (named after British Royal Navy battleships) is pictured on a charter photo stop in Blackpool, England, on May 23, 1978. This unique open-topped double-deck electric tram was built in 1902 by the Midland Railway Carriage & Wagon Company. It was overhauled in 1975 for the Borough of Blackpool's centenary celebrations in 1976 and was used in intermittent service including charters by groups and individuals. (*Kenneth C. Springirth photograph*)

Back cover: The April 4, 2010 Toronto Beaches Lions Club, on Queen Street between Wheeler Avenue and Lee Avenue, features Toronto streetcars PCC car No. 4549 (one of 100 cars [Nos. 4400–4499] built by St. Louis Car Company in 1949 and finished by Canadian Car & Foundry Company), Peter Witt car No. 2766 (one of fifty even-numbered cars [Nos. 2700–2798] built by Canadian Car & Foundry Company during 1922–1923), and Canadian Light Rail vehicle (CLRV) 4041 (one of 190 cars [Nos. 4010–4199] built by Hawker Siddeley Canada Limited with the first CLRVs going into service in 1979). (*Kenneth C. Springirth photograph*)

Fonthill Media Limited
Fonthill Media Inc.
www.fonthillmedia.com
office@fonthillmedia.com

First published in the United Kingdom
and the United States of America 2023

British Library Cataloguing in Publication Data:
A catalogue record for this book is available from the British Library

Copyright © Kenneth C. Springirth 2023

ISBN 978-1-62545-118-7

The right of Kenneth C. Springirth to be identified as the author of this work has been asserted by him in accordance with the Copyright, Designs and Patents Act 1988.

Typeset in Mrs Eaves XL Serif Narrow
Printed and bound in England

Contents

Acknowledgments

hanks to the Erie County (Pennsylvania) Public Library system for their knowledgeable and helpful staff. The author's wife Virginia Springirth who has been an outstanding wife, mother, plus has researched and photographed pictures over the years of trains and trolleys. Two pictures came from postcards (Used with permission from Audio Visual Designs [www.audiovisualdesigns.com]). Carl H. Sturner was the name of the photographer who took the pictures for those two postcards. Books that served as excellent reference sources were *Amsterdam Municipal Transport Facts and Figures for January 1, 1981; Fifty Years of Progressive Transit A History of the Toronto Transit Commission* by John F. Bromley and Jack May; *Hongkong Tramways A History of HongKong Tramways Limited* by R. L. P. Atkinson and A. K. Williams; *PCC Cars of North America* by Dr. Harold E. Cox; *The Tramways of Portugal A Visitor's Guide* by B. R. King and J. H. Price; *Tramways and Light Railways of Switzerland and Austria* by R. J. Buckley; and *Transit in the Triangle Volume I 1900–1964* by Blaine S. Hays and James A. Toman.

This book is dedicated to the author Kenneth C. Springirth's son, Philip Springirth, who, over the years, has an amazing way of solving technological challenges.

On July 5, 1979, Hong Kong Tramways colorful tram No. 124 (built by Hong Kong Tramways Limited and placed in service on March 23, 1951) has an array of advertising over the vehicle. (*Kenneth C. Springirth photograph*

Introduction

Pittsburgh along with Boston, Cleveland, New Orleans, Newark, Philadelphia, San Francisco, and Toronto are the only North American cities that have operated light rail systems that evolved uninterrupted from their original streetcar era. Pittsburgh's population dramatically increased from 49,221 in 1860 to 533,905 in 1910 as the steel industry and other industries rapidly expanded. Street railway systems expanded and the Second Avenue Traction Company completed the first electrified streetcar system in the Glenwood section of Pittsburgh. On January 1, 1902, Consolidated Traction Company and United Traction Company consolidated to become Pittsburgh Railways Company (PRC). The Mount Washington Tunnel Company was chartered by PRC to build a tunnel through Mount Washington to provide direct access from southern suburban areas to downtown Pittsburgh. On December 1, 1904, the Mount Washington Tunnel opened and was used by the Mount Washington, Dormont, Knoxville, Arlington, Beltzhoover, and Charleroi trolley routes. Pittsburgh Motor Coach Company, a separate division of PRC, was charted on July 27, 1925 and by the end of 1926 operated thirty-four buses on five routes. With ridership declining by 110 million between 1929 and 1933, on June 11, 1933, the elimination of all conductors was completed reducing operating expenses, and one-man cars provided all of the service.

In 1937, new Presidents' Conference Committee (PCC) cars were placed into service. By January 1938, with 201 PCC cars in service, PRC noted their rapid acceleration, smoothness of operation, and more comfortable seating resulted in increased ridership. On May 28, 1949, delivery was completed on 100 cars in the 1700 series PCC cars with PRC having a total of 666 PCC cars. On Sunday June 28, 1953 at 2 a.m., PCC car No. 1723 left Charleroi, Washington County, Pennsylvania, ending service on that interurban line. The line was cut back to Simmons Loop and renamed Route 35 Library. On August 29, 1953, the last run was made from Pittsburgh to Washington, Pennsylvania, and the line cut back to a new Drake Loop (designated Route 36 Drake located at McLaughlin Run & Drake Road in Upper St. Clair Township) that was placed in service on September 25, 1953. There were numerous trolley car line abandonments during 1952–1953, and the system became completely operated by PCC cars. On September 6, 1955, Route 38 Mt. Lebanon began using a new short-turn loop at 4th Avenue which provided faster outbound service from downtown Pittsburgh during rush hours.

Redevelopment in the City of Duquesne that would have required relocation of certain tracks used by trolley car routes 60 (East Liberty–Homestead) and 68 (Homestead–Duquesne–McKeesport) that the PRC determined would cost more than the trolley car routes were worth resulted in those lines converted to bus operation on September 20, 1958. With the opening of the Fort Pitt Bridge on June 19, 1959, on June 20, 1959, six remaining West End trolley car routes 25 (Island Avenue), 26 (West Park–McKees Rocks), 27 (Carnegie), 28 (Heidelberg), 30 (Crafton–Ingram), and 31/34 (Elliott–Sheraden) made their last runs. By 1962 the decline in ridership resulted in only about 300 PCC cars needed for rush hour service. PRC double tracked the connection between Route 38 (Mt. Lebanon) and 42 (Dormont) and combined them into Route 42/38 (Mt. Lebanon via Dormont and Beechview) on May 26, 1963. Route 77/54 (North Side–Carrick via Bloomfield) was cut back from the 22nd Street Bridge on July 7, 1963. High winds brought down wire and poles closing Route 98 (Glassport–McKeesport) on August 3, 1963. Route 56A (Lincoln Place via 2nd Avenue) and Route 56 (McKeesport via 2nd Avenue) made their last runs on August 31, 1963 with replacement by buses on September 1, 1963.

On February 29, 1964, the Court of Common Pleas permitted Port Authority Transit (PAT) to take over PRC. Effective July 5, 1964, trolley car Routes 22 (Crosstown), 55 (Homestead–East Pittsburgh), 57 (Glenwood), and 58 (Greenfield) were converted to bus operation. On September 5, 1965, trolley car Route 6 (Brighton Road) was combined with Route 13 (Emsworth) becoming Route 6/13 (Brighton/Emsworth); Northside trolley car routes 8 (Perrysville), 10 (Westview), and 15 (Bellevue) were converted to bus operation; plus East End trolley car routes 65 (Munhall–Lincoln Place) and 77/54 (North Side–Carrick via Bloomfield) became bus routes. On December 31, 1965, Route 6/13 (Brighton/Emsworth) was cut back to the Avalon Loop due to deterioration of the Ben Avon and Avalon trolley car bridges and became Route 6/14 (Brighton–Avalon). Northside trolley Routes 6/14 Brighton–Avalon) and 21 (Fineview) made their last runs on April 31, 1966. Route 85 (Bedford) converted to bus operation on June 26, 1966. South Hills trolley car Routes 39 (Brookline) and 40 (Mount Washington) were converted to bus operation on September 4, 1966. East end Routes 64, 66, 67, 71, 73, 75, 76, 82, 87, and 88 were converted to bus operation on January 29, 1967. Route 48 (Arlington) was replaced by a bus route extension on March 31, 1968. Routes 44 (Knoxville), 49 (Beltzhoover), and 53 (Carrick) made their final runs early Sunday morning November 14, 1971.

DOUBLE DECK CAR, LARGEST IN THE WORLD—SEATS 110 PEOPLE. PITTSBURGH, PA.

In this postcard postmarked September 6, 1921, Pittsburgh Railways Company (PRC) double-truck, double-end, and double-deck trolley car No. 6001 is on Route 73 waiting for departure time. This was one of six cars (Nos. 6000–6005) built by St. Louis Car Company in 1913.

On April 21, 1963, sharp-looking Presidents' Conference Committee (PCC) car No. 1705 is on the siding at Library Loop for a trolley car excursion photo stop. PRC had repainted this car in a simplified paint scheme. This was one of seventy-five cars (Nos. 1700–1775) built by St. Louis Car Company and delivered to PRC during December 1947 to May 1948. Powered by four Westinghouse type 1432 motors, the car seated fifty passengers and weighed 37,500 pounds. (*Kenneth C. Springirth photograph*)

1

Pittsburgh, Pennsylvania, United States, Light Rail System

Most of Pittsburgh's trolley car lines had been converted to bus operation. Sunday morning November 14, 1971 the four surviving trolley car routes were 35 (Library), 36 (Drake), 37 (Shannon), and 42/38 (Mt. Lebanon–Beechview). There was opposition in the southern suburbs to a proposed Skybus system. Community and civic leaders favored saving the four surviving trolley car lines. Following extensive discussion, light rail was adopted for the southern suburbs. On May 7, 1979, Port Authority Transit (PAT) was awarded a $265 million federal grant to upgrade 10.5 miles of the rail line of which 1.1 miles would be a downtown subway to eliminate the trolley car's slow street-running loop in downtown Pittsburgh. On December 10, 1980 after receiving federal funding, PAT began Stage One of the project which included the downtown subway and the former trolley route from a newly constructed South Hill Village Station and Light Rail Maintenance Center to Castle Shannon. Fifty-five new light rail cars (Nos. 4201–4255), Model SD400 built by Siemens Duewag, began operating from South Hills Village to Castle Shannon on April 15, 1984. The last day of trolley car service on downtown Pittsburgh streets and across the Smithfield Street Bridge was July 6, 1985. The subway opened for full service on July 7, 1985. When the line leaves the subway, it crosses the Monongahela River via the refurbished former Pennsylvania Railroad Panhandle Bridge.

The section from Castle Shannon via Mt. Lebanon and Beechview was approved for $20 million in federal funding on May 8, 1985. In Beechview, the Fallowfield Bridge was completely rebuilt. Beneath Washington Road from McFarland Road to Shady Drive East, the 3,000-foot-long Dormont/Mount Lebanon Tunnel was constructed linking Dormont and Mount Lebanon stations. The rebuilt line opened on May 22, 1987 retaining the street-level stops in Beechview and operates to South Hills Village. PCC cars continued to serve the Overbrook Line which operated from South Hills Junction via Overbrook to Castle Shannon. Sixteen PCC cars were rebuilt, of which twelve were completely rebuilt with new propulsion and braking systems. The four partially rebuilt cars kept their original interior and exterior lighting, operator's controls, and retained their original numbers.

From 1984 to 1993, rehabilitated PCC trolley cars operated on the Overbrook line. With the deterioration of the Overbrook Line, Route 47 (Shannon) was taken out of service on June 3, 1993. Route 47D, operating between Drake and Castle Shannon, was the only remaining PCC car line, and was later cut back to operate from Drake to Washington Junction. When PCC car service ended on September 4, 1999, the Drake Line was closed. On September 5, 1999, a final excursion was conducted using the last remaining PAT PCC cars Nos. 4004 (ex-1739), 4008 (ex-1709), and 4009 (ex-1700). This closed out Pittsburgh's sixty-three years of PCC car service which began when PCC car No. 100 was delivered in July 1936. Rebuilding of the Overbrook Line began in 1999. It was a new line built on the original line's right of way completely double tracked with new catenary, new signaling, and eight high-level platform ADA accessible stations. To service this line and increase overall system capacity, twenty-eight new light rail vehicles (Nos. 4301–4328) were purchased from Construcciones Y Auxiliar de Ferrocarriles S.A. (CAF) which in English means "Construction & Other Railway Services" and went into service during 2003–2004.

Route 52, later known as the Brown Line, once operated from South Hills Junction via Warrington Avenue and Arlington Avenue and across the Monongahela River to downtown Pittsburgh. This was the only remaining trolley line that did not serve Station Square and did not use the Mount Washington Transit Tunnel. While this line was discontinued in the March 27, 2011 system-wide cuts, the track and overhead wire are in place so it can be used as a bypass when the Mount Washington Transit Tunnel is closed for maintenance or emergencies.

With federal funding assistance, PAT began construction to extend the line from downtown Pittsburgh's Gateway Station with twin bored tunnels under the Allegheny River to Allegheny Station. Tunneling began in January 2008. The completed extension opened on March 25, 2012. The COVID-19 pandemic has resulted in a significant decline in public transit ridership. With the ability to work from home, many workers have not returned to using public transit. Looking at the American Public Transportation (APTA) Light Rail Fourth Quarter 2019 Report and Light Rail Fourth Quarter 2020 Report, PAT ridership from October 2019 to December 2019 was 1,850,100 and declined 81.29 percent to 346,200 for October 2020 to December 2020. The APTA Light Rail Fourth Quarter 2021 Report shows PAT ridership from October 2021 to December 2021 was 626,600 which was an increase of 81.29 percent, but is significantly lower than the October 2019 to December 2019 total.

In a June 9, 2022 news release, Port Authority Transit is now Pittsburgh Regional Transit (PRT). Schedules, brochures, website, signage, and new vehicles will be redesigned to reflect PRT.

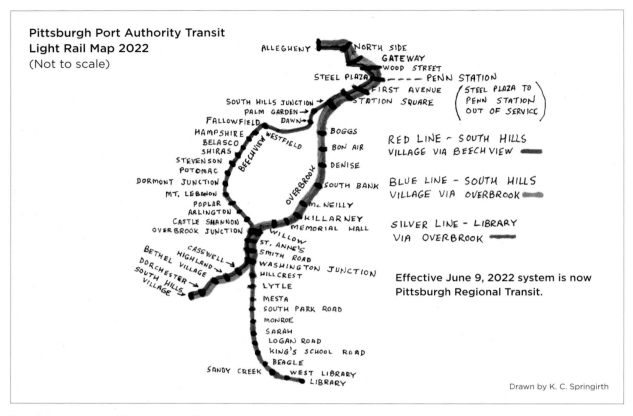

Pittsburgh Port Authority Transit
Light Rail Map 2022
(Not to scale)

ALLEGHENY — NORTH SIDE
GATEWAY
WOOD STREET
STEEL PLAZA — — — PENN STATION
FIRST AVENUE
SOUTH HILLS JUNCTION → STATION SQUARE
PALM GARDEN →
FALLOWFIELD   DAWN →
HAMPSHIRE   WESTFIELD   BOGGS
BELASCO
SHIRAS   BON AIR
STEVENSON
POTOMAC   DENISE
DORMONT JUNCTION   SOUTH BANK
MT. LEBANON
POPLAR   McNEILLY
ARLINGTON   KILLARNEY
CASTLE SHANNON   MEMORIAL HALL
OVERBROOK JUNCTION   WILLOW
CASWELL   ST. ANNE'S
BETHEL   HIGHLAND →   SMITH ROAD
VILLAGE   WASHINGTON JUNCTION
DORCHESTER   HILLCREST
SOUTH HILLS   LYTLE
VILLAGE →
MESTA
SOUTH PARK ROAD
MONROE
SARAH
LOGAN ROAD
KING'S SCHOOL ROAD
BEAGLE
SANDY CREEK   WEST LIBRARY
LIBRARY

BEECHVIEW
OVERBROOK

(STEEL PLAZA TO
PENN STATION
OUT OF SERVICE)

RED LINE – SOUTH HILLS
VILLAGE VIA BEECHVIEW ▬

BLUE LINE – SOUTH HILLS
VILLAGE VIA OVERBROOK ▬

SILVER LINE – LIBRARY
VIA OVERBROOK ▬

Effective June 9, 2022 system is now
Pittsburgh Regional Transit.

Drawn by K. C. Springirth

The above map shows PRT operates a 25.2-mile system with three light rail lines: Red Line from South Hills Village via Beechview to Allegheny Station; Blue Line from South Hills Village via South Bank Station (Overbrook) to Allegheny Station; and Silver Line from Library via South Bank Station (Overbrook) to Allegheny Station.

On June 27, 1973, South Hills Junction yard is the location of Port Authority Transit (PAT) Presidents' Conference Committee (PCC) car No. 1730 painted in a psychedelic paint scheme. This was one of seventy-five PCC cars (Nos. 1700–1774) built by St. Louis Car Company and delivered during December 1947 to May 1948. (*Kenneth C. Springirth photograph*)

PAT Refurbished PCC car No. 1787 (originally car No. 1628 one of seventy-four PCC cars [Nos. 1601–1674] built by St. Louis Car Company and delivered during August to October 1945) is arriving at the P&LE Railroad Station stop on Smithfield Street in downtown Pittsburgh on July 21, 1980 on a southbound Route 42/38 Mount Lebanon/Beechview trip. (*Kenneth C. Springirth photograph*)

On July 21, 1980, PAT Route 42/38 PCC car No. 1751 (one of seventy-five cars [Nos. 1700–1774] built by St. Louis Car Company and delivered during December 1947 to May 1948) has arrived at the P&LE Station. Constructed in 1898, the P&LE Station was used as a passenger station by the Pittsburgh & Lake Erie (P&LE) Railroad. The Baltimore & Ohio Railroad also used this station for some of its passenger trains. (*Kenneth C. Springirth photograph*)

South Hills Junction (west of the Liberty Tunnel and accessed from W. Warrington Avenue north of its intersection with Saw Mill Run Boulevard) is the location of PAT PCC car No. 1745 on May 17, 1983. In the 1970s and 1980s, Pittsburgh's trolley cars were painted in a rainbow of colors. (*Photographer Carl H. Sturner Used with permission from Audio Visual Designs [www.audiovisualdesigns.com]*)

PAT Route 47 Shannon PCC car No. 1765 is at the Castle Shannon Loop in the Borough of Castle Shannon in Allegheny County, on July 3, 1989. This car along with cars Nos. 1713, 1737, and 1745 received extensive rehabilitation; however, they retained their original configuration and original number. (*Kenneth C. Springirth photograph*)

On July 25, 1998, PAT Light Rail Vehicle (LRV) No. 4111 is at South Hills Junction on a Route 52 (Allentown) trip. There were fifty-five of these double-ended articulated type SD-400 cars (Nos. 4101–4155) built during 1985–1987 by Siemens Duewag. Empty weight of the 84.67-foot-long car is 85,800 pounds. With Pittsburgh having a mix of high-level and low-level platform stops, each car has three high-level double-stream doors per side and one low-level single-stream door opposite the operator's area at either end. Each car seated sixty-two and had a standing capacity of 218 passengers. (*Kenneth C. Springirth photograph*)

Completely rebuilt PAT PCC car No. 4004 (originally car No. 1739) is at Castle Shannon on July 25, 1998. (*Kenneth C. Springirth photograph*)

On June 5, 2022, the PAT South Hills Village Rail Center, near the South Hills Village Mall, is the location of LRV No. 4222 (originally Siemens Duewag SD-400 car No. 4122, rebuilt by CAF, and renumbered 4222) that was repainted on October 5, 2014 to resemble the PCC cars that once served Pittsburgh plus commemorate the fiftieth anniversary of Port Authority Transit (PAT) which acquired Pittsburgh Railways in 1964. (*Kenneth C. Springirth photograph*)

From left to right over the inspection pits at the PAT South Hills Village Rail Center on June 5, 2022 are LRVs No. 4314 (built by CAF) and No. 4226 (originally Siemens Duewag SD-400 No. 4126, refurbished by CAF, and renumbered 4226). LRVs and some maintenance of way vehicles are stored at this facility. (*Kenneth C. Springirth photograph*)

LRV No. 4213 (originally Siemens Duewag SD-400 No. 4113, refurbished by CAF, and renumbered 4213) is parked over the well-designed repair pit at the PAT South Hills Village Rail Center on June 5, 2022. (*Kenneth C. Springirth photograph*)

On June 5, 2022, an upper-viewing level at the PAT South Hills Village Rail Center provides an overall view from left to right of LRVs No. 4213 (originally No. 4113) and No. 4227 (originally No. 4127) with wheel sets and other LRV parts ready for use. Just as consumers faced challenges over supply chain issues in 2022, transit authorities also faced challenges in getting the parts needed to keep transit vehicles in service. (*Kenneth C. Springirth photograph*)

LRV No. 4243 (originally No. 4143) in a colorful advertising theme is on the inspection track at the PAT South Hills Village Rail Center on June 5, 2022. Today's modern light rail vehicles are more complicated than the PCC cars they replaced. (*Kenneth C. Springirth photograph*)

On June 5, 2022, from left to right, LRVs built by CAF No. 4325, 4327, and 4324 are at the outdoor yard of the PAT South Hills Village Rail Center in this continuing year of medical concerns and facing delays plus higher costs in getting replacement parts. (*Kenneth C. Springirth photograph*)

On June 23, 2022, a Pittsburgh Regional Transit (PRT), the new name for Port Authority Transit which went into effect on June 9, 2022, motorized truck used for overhead wire work, is at the South Hills Village Station (in Bethel Park, Pennsylvania, adjacent to the South Hills Village shopping complex) examining the overhead wire. (*Kenneth C. Springirth photograph*)

PRT LRV No. 4211 (originally No. 4111) is at South Hills Junction about to make the turn into the Mount Washington Transit Tunnel for a northbound trip to downtown Pittsburgh on June 23, 2022. The type SD-400 cars (originally numbered 4101–4155) were refurbished during 2005–2006 and were renumbered 4201–4255. (*Kenneth C. Springirth photograph*)

Under a June 23, 2022 clear blue sky, refurbished Siemens Duewag LRV No. 4202 (originally No. 4102) is on a northbound PRT Red Line trip on Broadway Avenue at Coast Avenue in Beechview, a neighborhood in the southwestern part of Pittsburgh. (*Kenneth C. Springirth photograph*)

Northbound refurbished Siemens Duewag LRV No. 4251 (originally No. 4151) is in the borough of Dormont in Allegheny County at Stevenson Station on the PRT middle of the road private right of section of the Red Line on June 23, 2022. (*Kenneth C. Springirth photograph*)

On June 23, 2022, refurbished LRV No. 4247 (originally car No. 4147) is on a PRT southbound Red Line trip approaching Stevenson Station. The Red Line exhibits just about every possible right of way a light rail line can have including a tunnel under Washington Road in Mount Lebanon from Shady Drive to McFarland Road, private median at Stevenson Station, street running in the middle of Broadway Avenue, private right of way including sections squeezed between backyards with many grade crossings, Mount Washington Transit Tunnel, and the downtown Pittsburgh subway. (*Kenneth C. Springirth photograph*)

Washington Junction in Bethel Park is the location of northbound PRT refurbished LRV No. 4211 (originally car No. 4111) that is going into rush hour service on the Blue Line on June 23, 2022. This station has a commuter park and ride facility plus is used as a transfer point for Red, Blue, and Silver Line passengers. (*Kenneth C. Springirth photograph*)

Northbound PRT car No. 4309 (one of twenty-eight LRVs [Nos. 4301–4328] built by CAF during 2003–2004 with each LRV having a total passenger capacity of 264) on June 23, 2022 is passing the Dorchester Station which serves the nearby Dorchester Apartment complex in Bethel Park. (*Kenneth C. Springirth photograph*)

PRT refurbished LRV No. 4250 (originally car No. 4150) is southbound gliding by the Dorchester Station on June 23, 2022 heading for the next station which is the terminus at South Hills Village. (*Kenneth C. Springirth photograph*)

2
Toronto, Canada, Streetcars

Toronto Street Railway Company opened its first horse-drawn streetcar line on Queen Street from King to Bloor with a track gauge of 4 feet 10.875 inches on September 11, 1861. The company was sold to a new company which on April 14, 1892 incorporated as the Toronto Railway Company (TRC) and placed the first electric trolley car in service on Church Street on August 15, 1892. Toronto's last horse car ended service on McCaul Street on August 31, 1894. To stimulate development of outlying areas, the city began developing the Toronto Civic Railways. Concerned over lack of public transit in new areas, on January 1, 1920, voters approved the city taking over TRC. A "commission" form of management was established rather than have a street railway department that would be subject to political interference. The Toronto Transportation Commission (TTC) came into existence on June 4, 1920.

Based on the success of the Peter Witt streetcar design in Cleveland, 100 new trolley cars and sixty trailer cars were ordered on April 27, 1921 from Canadian Car & Foundry Company Limited of Montreal. In August 1921, the first new Peter Witt cars (Nos. 2300 and 2302) were displayed at the Canadian National Exhibition. On September 1, 1921, the TTC took over operation of both the TRC and the Toronto Civic Railway.

TTC ridership reached 206,882,838 in 1929; however, during the Depression, this declined to 147,582,487 in 1933. The TTC ordered 140 PCC cars (Nos. 4000–4139) constructed by the St. Louis Car Company and to save on expensive import duties on completed cars were finished at the Canadian Car & Foundry plant in Montreal, Canada. On September 24, 1938, the St. Clair line became the first TTC route to be completely operated by PCC cars. During the 1939–1945 World War II years, there was a significant increase in public transit ridership. Need to divert gasoline, oil, and rubber to win World War II temporarily halted the growth of the automobile and motor bus. After the war ended, streetcars on the Sherbourne line made their last runs on January 4, 1947, and the line was converted to bus operation. Trolley coaches replaced streetcars on the Lansdowne line on June 19, 1947. The Dovercourt streetcar line was replaced on December 8, 1947 on the south end by the Ossington trolley coach line and the northern portion by a rerouted Harbord line. On July 25, 1949, the first of the 100 Class A7 4000-series multiple-unit-equipped PCC cars arrived at the Hillcrest Shops and began revenue multiple unit operation on the Bloor Danforth line on August 30, 1949. There were fifty-two PCC cars purchased from Cincinnati Railway on July 28, 1950 which became Nos. 4550–4601. Birmingham Electric Company

sold forty-eight PCC cars to TTC which became Nos. 4700–4747. Cleveland Transit sold seventy-five PCC cars to TTC which became Nos. 4625–4699. Kansas City Public Service Company sold thirty PCC cars to TTC which became Nos. 4750–4779.

With the opening of the Yonge Street Subway on March 30, 1954, the Bay and Yonge streetcar lines were abandoned. The University Subway opened on February 28, 1963, and the Dupont streetcar line was abandoned. On February 26, 1966, the Bloor–Danforth subway opened, and the MU operated Bloor–Danforth streetcar line was abandoned except for two short streetcar segments (one at each end of the line). The Harbord, Fort, Parliament, and Coxwell streetcar lines were abandoned. Kingston Road–Coxwell and Bathurst–Downtown routes were discontinued with all Bathurst cars operating to the Exhibition. Operation of the Bathurst line north of Bathurst Station at Bloor Street except for pullins and pullouts was replaced by extensions of the Bathurst and Vaughan buses.

On May 11, 1968, the Bloor–Danforth Subway extensions opened. The Dundas streetcar line was cut back to the Dundas West Station. The Danforth streetcar shuttle at the east end was replaced by the subway extension.

On June 22, 1990, the TTC opened the Route 604 (Harbourfront) streetcar line from Union Station via Queens Way to Spadina Avenue. It became Route 510 on February 18, 1996, and track was laid on Spadina Avenue to an underground terminal at the Spadina Subway Station. The expanded Route 510 streetcar line opened on July 27, 1997 replacing the former Route 77 Spadina bus. Spadina originally was a streetcar line from Bloor Street to Fleet Street that had been converted to bus operation on October 10, 1948.

Trackage along Queens Quay was constructed from Spadina Avenue to Bathurst Street and north on Bathurst Street to Fleet Street joining the Bathurst Streetcar line at Fleet Street. Route 509 (Harbourfront) opened on July 21, 2000 linking Union Station with Exhibition Loop. Streetcar Route 512 (St. Clair) was rebuilt to have a private right of way in the median of St. Clair Avenue which was completed on June 30, 2010.

With public support for continued streetcar service, the TTC ordered a new Canadian Light Rail Vehicle (CLRV) to replace the PCC cars. The first six of these cars (Nos. 4000–4005) were manufactured by Schweizerische Industrie Gesellschaft (Swiss Industrial Company or SIG) of Zurich, Switzerland, and would serve as models for the Urban Transportation Development Corporation (UTDC). From 1977 to 1981, 196 CLRVs were built. The last regular service PCC car operated on December 8, 1995. There were fifty-two Articulated Light Rail Vehicles (ALRVs)

(Nos. 4200–4251) built by MAN (Maschinenfabrik Augsburg-Nurnberg) of Germany and the UTDC during 1987–1989. ALRV No. 4204 was the first to be placed in service on Route 507 (Long Branch) on January 19, 1988. In 2006, CLRV No. 4041 received an air-conditioning unit installed on its roof. It was a prototype for a refurbishment project that was cancelled. The 2005 Canadian Accessibility for Ontarians with Disabilities Act affected the high-floor CLRV and ALRV fleet, because it was not possible to make them fully accessible. As the CLRV/ALRV fleet aged, its propulsion control system became unreliable, and it became difficult to obtain replacement parts. Cold winter weather resulted in water vapor freezing in the pneumatic air lines, preventing brakes and doors from functioning. All ALRVs were removed from service on September 3, 2019 followed by CLRVs on December 29, 2019.

Back in 2007, the TTC began looking at replacing the CLRV/ALRV fleet. In 2009, the TTC announced it had chosen a customized version of the Bombardier Flexity Outlook to replace the streetcar fleet. The new vehicle features a low floor design, a loading ramp for wheelchair access, doubling of passenger capacity, air conditioning, and electronic destination signs at the front, side, and rear of the vehicle. Bombardier had manufacturing and quality control problems mainly with welding at one of its plants. The final vehicle of the 204 car order, No. 4603, arrived at the Hillcrest Complex from Bombardier's Thunder Bay plant on January 24, 2020. The first two Bombardier Flexity streetcars went into service on Route 510 (Spadina) on August 31, 2014, and these new streetcars began operating from the new Leslie Barns maintenance and storage facility on November 22, 2015. Route 514 (Cherry) was inaugurated on June 19, 2016 to supplement Route 514 (King) service along King Street between Dufferin and Sumach Streets. The eastern end of Route 514 operated on a newly constructed line originally named Cherry Street streetcar line. On September 12, 2017, Route 509 (Harbourfront) became the first Toronto streetcar route to operate Bombardier streetcars with electrical pickup by pantograph instead of by trolley pole. On October 7, 2018, Route 514 (Cherry) was replaced by a realignment of Route 504 into two overlapping branches. Route 504A operated from Dundas West Station via Roncesvalles Avenue, King, and Cherry Street to Distillery Loop. Route 504B operated from Dufferin Gate Loop via Dufferin Street, King Street, Queen Street, and Broadview Avenue to Broadway Station. The two branches overlapped on King Street between Dufferin Street and Cherry Street.

On September 2, 2019, the TTC retired the last of the ALRV streetcars. With construction work at the Queen, Kingston Road, and Eastern Avenue intersection, the TTC eliminated Route 502 Downtowner service, and the 503 Kingston Road rush-hour service began operating daytime hours Monday through Friday. On December 29, 2019, the TTC retired the last of the CLRVs, and all TTC streetcar service was now by Bombardier vehicles.

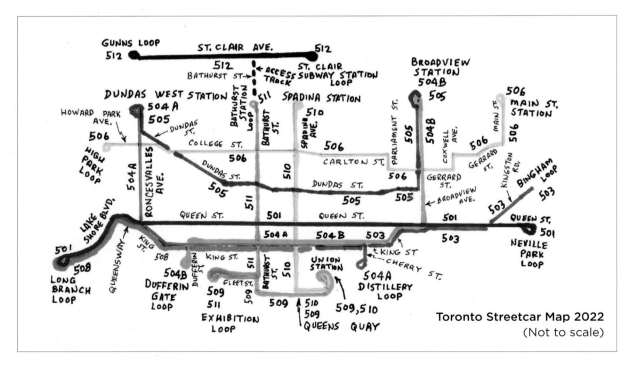

The above map shows the following Toronto Transit Commission (TTC) streetcar routes in 2022: 501 Queen (Long Branch Loop–Neville Park Loop), 503 Kingston Road (University Ave./York St.–Bingham Loop), 504A King (Dundas W. Station–Distillery Loop), 504B (Duffern Gate Loop–Broadview Station), 505 Dundas (Dundas W. Station–Broadview Station), 506 Carlton (High Park Loop–Main St. Station), 508 Lake Shore (Long Branch Loop–King St. downtown Toronto morning rush hour and in the afternoon rush hour from King & Church to Long Branch Loop), 509 Harbourfront (Exhibition Loop–Union Station), 510 Spadina (Spadina Station–Union Station), 511 Bathurst (Bathurst Station–Exhibition Loop), and 512 St. Clair (Gunns Loop–St. Clair Station).

On June 23, 2007, Route 510 Canadian Light Rail Vehicle (CLRV) No. 4107, in an advertising paint scheme, is southbound on Spadina Avenue crossing the grand union at Queen Street where there are two double tracks crossing at grade with sixteen switches in place to allow a streetcar to go straight or make a right or left turn from any approach track. Toronto's two other grand unions are on King Street at Spadina Avenue and King Street at Bathurst Street. When the CLRVs were introduced, there was wheel noise which was solved by changing from Bocham wheels (which had rubber in compression) to SAB wheels (which had rubber in shear). Passengers praised the CLRVs for their smooth ride, bright fluorescent lighting, and large windows. (*Kenneth C. Springirth photograph*)

ALRV No. 4215 is on Queen Street at John Street in downtown Toronto for a westbound trip Route 501 (Queen) trip to Long Branch on June 23, 2007. The 15.4-mile Route 501 is the longest streetcar route in Canada stretching from Long Branch Loop east via Lake Shore Boulevard, with private right of way in the median of the Queensway, and street running on Queen Street to its eastern terminus at Neville Park Loop. (*Kenneth C. Springirth photograph*)

On a cloudy bright June 23, 2007, Route 505 CLRV No. 4195 is on a diversion route turning from College Street and heading south on Ossington Avenue where it will turn east on Dundas Street to return on its normal route via Dundas Street and Broadview Avenue to Broadview Station. Route 505 is normally a U-shaped line connecting Dundas West Station via Roncesvalles Avenue, Dundas Street, and Broadview Avenue to Broadview Station. (*Kenneth C. Springirth photograph*)

Well-maintained President's Conference Committee (PCC) car No. 4500 is at the Fleet Street Loop on August 2, 2009. The front sign displays, "This 1951 streetcar has been restored by the proud employees of the TTC." Fifty PCC cars (Nos. 4500–4549) Toronto Class A8 had the body shell built by St. Louis Car Company and were finished by Canadian Car & Foundry Company. These cars were ordered in March 1950 and delivered in January–March 1951. Each car was powered by four Westinghouse type 1432 motors. (*Kenneth C. Springirth photograph*)

tppe="

On September 6, 2009, PCC car No. 4500 is on King Street at Spadina Avenue. Note the special wording, "The TTC welcomes you to Toronto." (*Kenneth C. Springirth photograph*)

Spadina Avenue at Nassau Street finds CLRV No. 4013 signed to short turn at Dundas Street on July 22, 2011. The CLRV did not become the leading vehicle in the streetcar rebirth. For example, Boston borrowed three CLRVs (Nos. 4027, 4029, and 4031) for testing; however, Boston also purchased a Japanese-designed streetcar. (*Kenneth C. Springirth photograph*)

Route 501 ALRV No. 4231 is on its eastbound trip to Neville Park Loop using the Queen Street bridge to cross over the Don River, Don Valley Parkway, and the Go Transit Richmond Hill line which operates between Union Station in Toronto and the Bloomington Go Station in Richmond Hill on July 22, 2011. (*Kenneth C. Springirth photograph*)

On August 28, 2011, in a smartly painted advertising theme, CLRV No. 4123 is eastbound on Queens Quay at Dan Leckie Way on a Route 509 (Harbourfront) trip to Union Station. Route 509 began service on June 22, 1990 as Route 604 (Harbourfront) and with the completion of streetcar track on Spadina Avenue in 1997 became Route 510 (Spadina). (*Kenneth C. Springirth photograph*)

Near the front of the April 8, 2012 Toronto Beaches Lions Club Easter Parade on Queen Street at Glen Manor is TTC Peter Witt car No. 2766 (built by Canadian Car & Foundry in 1922) with CLRV No. 4074 behind it. Initially Peter Witt streetcars were the workhorse of the TTC's streetcar fleet. With arrival of PCC cars and later trimming of streetcar routes, the number of Peter Witt cars declined. The final Peter Witt car No. 2766 was kept in active duty until July 18, 1965 when it was used for a retirement fan trip. In 2002–2003, it received a major rebuilding and repainting. It was wonderful to witness the smiles on the faces of the parade-goers as this car operated on Queen Street. (*Kenneth C. Springirth photograph*)

On April 20, 2014, immaculate-looking TTC streetcars PCC car No. 4549, Peter Witt car No. 2766, CLRV No. 4186, and Flexity Outlook Light Rail Vehicle No. 4402 are on Queen Street at Hambly Avenue for the April 20, 2014 Toronto Beaches Lions Club Easter Parade. (*Kenneth C. Springirth photograph*)

Hundreds of spectators are on both sides of Queen Street at Herbert Street as the last two TTC streetcars CLRV No. 4186 and Flexity Outlook Light Rail Vehicle No. 4402 pass by on April 20, 2014. (*Kenneth C. Springirth photograph*)

On July 15, 2018, Route 501 CLRV No. 4189, heading for Long Branch, is making a passenger stop on Lake Shore Boulevard at Royal York Road. This car was removed for scrap on October 18, 2019. (*Kenneth C. Springirth photograph*)

Route 512 (St. Clair) Flexity Outlook Light Rail Vehicle No. 4414 is at Gunns Loop waiting for departure time on July 15, 2018. This car was delivered to the TTC Hillcrest Shop on December 14, 2015 and entered service on December 24, 2015 on Route 510. The car was sent back to Bombardier for repairs on September 6, 2019. It was sent back to the TTC on June 30, 2020. (*Kenneth C. Springirth photograph*)

On July 15, 2018, Route 512 Flexity Outlook Light Rail Vehicle No. 4445 is on St. Clair Avenue at Weston Road. Delivered to the TTC Hillcrest Shop on September 19, 2017, this car went into service on October 5, 2017 on Route 514. It went back to Bombardier for repairs on November 16, 2021, and was returned to the TTC on February 1, 2022. (*Kenneth C. Springirth photograph*)

Queen Street at University Avenue is the location of Route 501 Flexity Outlook Light Rail Vehicle No. 4441. Hillcrest Shop received this car on August 3, 2017 and went into service on August 25, 2017 on Route 509. It was returned to Bombardier for repairs on October 5, 2021 and was returned the TTC on February 22, 2022. It was returned to service on Route 510 on March 22, 2022. (*Kenneth C. Springirth photograph*)

On September 23, 2018, Route 501 Flexity Outlook Light Rail Vehicle No. 4460 with Canadian Light Rail Vehicle (CLRV) No. 4153 (less than a year later, it was removed for scrap in July 2019) behind it are at Humber Loop. Car No. 4460 was received by Hillcrest Shop on January 2, 2018 and entered service on January 17, 2018 on Route 510. It went back to Bombardier for repairs on April 12, 2022. (*Kenneth C. Springirth photograph*)

3
Manx Electric Railway, Snaefell Mountain Railway, & Douglas Horse Tramway

The Manx Electric Railway began construction in 1893 of a single-track 2.5-mile electric tramway from the northern terminus of the Douglas horse tramway on the Isle of Man at Derby Castle in the town of Douglas to Groudle Glen. Before the line opened, a new company, Douglas & Laxey Coast Electric Railway formed on March 7, 1893 to take over the line and extend it to Laxey. On March 30, 1894, the name became Isle of Man Railways & Electric Power Company, and opened to Laxey on July 28, 1894. Laxey to Ramsey opened on August 2, 1898, and the final extension to the center of Ramsey opened on July 24, 1899 making it a 17-mile line from Douglas to Ramsey. On November 12, 1902, the Manx Electric Railway Company was incorporated and purchased the line the next day. After World War II, the company struggled financially, and on June 1, 1957, ownership of the railway was sold to the Isle of Man Government for about its scrap value. A government board was formed to manage the line which became known as the Isle of Man Passenger Transport Board. In September 1975, the railway lost the mail contract, and the Laxey to Ramsey section was taken out of service. After public protest, Laxey to Ramsey service was restored in 1977. Between November 2007 and March 2008, 5.6 kilometers of track was rehabilitated, reusing as many of the existing rails as possible laid over new ballast and sleepers. A sleeper is a railroad tie in the United States. The Laxey to Ramsey section closed again in summer of 2008, reopened in 2009, and remained in operation except for a COVID-related suspension.

The 3-foot 6-inch gauge Snaefell Mountain Railway was the idea of the Snaefell Mountain Railway Association (SMRA) who hired the contractors for the construction which took place between January and August 1895 with the official public opening on August 21, 1895. Having successfully built and operated their railway, the SMRA sold the entire line to the Isle of Man Tramways & Electric Company in December 1895. The line was extended in 1896 to a new low-level station that provided a connection with the Manx Electric Railway at Laxey and made the Snaefell Mountain Railway 4.9 miles long. During World War II, the line closed on September 20, 1939 and reopened on June 1, 1946. The line was nationalized by the Isle of Man Government on June 1, 1957. Car No. 1 was re-equipped with new trucks in June 1977. Cars Nos. 2 and 3 received new trucks in the winter of 1977 followed by cars Nos. 4, 5, and 6 in 1978.

The 1.6-mile, 3-foot narrow-gauge Douglas Bay Horse Tram opened in 1876 and was built and operated by civil engineer Thomas Lightfoot. In 1882, Lightfoot sold the line to the Isle of Man Tramways & Electric Power Company which went into liquidation in 1900. The horse tram line was sold to the Douglas Corporation in 1902, and since 1927 operated only in the summer. In January 2016, as a result of substantial losses, the Douglas Corporation announced the horse tram line had closed. After an online petition received more than 2,000 signatures, the horse tram operation was taken over by the Isle of Man Heritage Railways division of the Department of Infrastructure and restored operation as a heritage transport service. In 2022, service operated from July 30 to October 30 from Derby Castle to Villa Marina.

The map shows the Isle of Man which features the Douglas Bay Horse Tramway, Manx Electric Railway, and the Snaefell Mountain Railway.

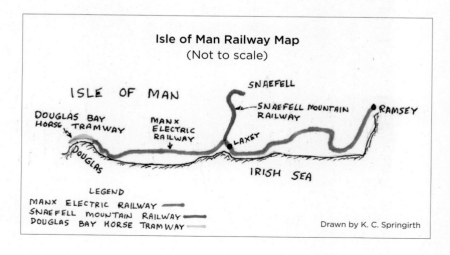

Drawn by K. C. Springirth

Manx Electric Railway fifty-six-passenger open-cross bench car No. 32 is seen here in a June 1, 1978 photo stop on the Isle of Man. Powered by four General Electric type 60 motors, this car (chartered by the author of this book Kenneth Springirth) was built in 1906 by the United Electric Car Company of Preston, England. In 1957, the line became known as the Isle of Man Railways. The word "Heritage" was added in 2009 making it the Isle of Man Heritage Railways. (*Kenneth C. Springirth photograph*)

On June 1, 1978, Manx Electric Railway car No. 5 in a red, white, and teak paint scheme is waiting for departure time at Derby Castle Station. Built in 1894 by G.F. Milnes & Company in Birkenhead (later of Hadley Castle, England) with four motors built by Societe l'Electricite et l'Hydraulique of Charleroi, Belgium. This car seated thirty-six passengers. (*Kenneth C. Springirth photograph*)

Manx Electric Railway car No. 26 with pole up is ready for the next assignment on May 29, 1978. Seating fifty-six passengers, this car was built in 1898 by G.F. Milnes & Company and powered by four motors built by Societe l'Electricite et l'Hydraulique of Charleroi, Belgium. This is the oldest tramline in the world, whose original rolling stock is still in service. (*Kenneth C. Springirth photograph*)

On May 29, 1978, Manx Electric Railway car No. 20 (seating forty-eight people), with a trailer behind it, is ready for the next trip. This car was built in 1899 by G.F. Milnes & Company, powered by four motors built by Societe l'Electricite et l'Hydraulique of Charleroi, Belgium. (*Kenneth C. Springirth photograph*)

At the base of Snaefell Mountain in the mountainous northern part of the Isle of Man, car No. 5 in a red, white, and teak paint scheme is ready for the next trip up the 2,036-foot-high Snaefell Mountain on May 30, 1978. This was one of six cars (Nos. 1–6) built by G.F. Milnes & Company for the Snaefell Mountain Railway. (*Kenneth C. Springirth photograph*)

Snaefell Mountain Railway car No. 6 is at the top of Snaefell Mountain on May 30, 1978. A loaded Snaefell Mountain car with forty-eight seated passengers and twelve standing passengers weighing about 15 tons could climb the line's gradient at a speed of about 10 miles per hour. The trip takes thirty minutes in each direction. (*Kenneth C. Springirth photograph*)

On May 31, 1978, Douglas Bay Horse Tramway car No. 28 in Douglas, Isle of Man, with the author's daughters Kathy and Grace Springirth looking out the front windows at the beginning point of their chartered trip organized by their parents Virginia and Kenneth Springirth. This car, seating thirty, was built by G.F. Milnes & Company in 1892 and was sold in August 2016. (*Kenneth C. Springirth photograph*)

The promenade in Douglas, Isle of Man, is the location of Douglas Bay Horse Tramway open car No. 35 on May 28, 1978. Seating thirty-two passengers, this car was built by G.F. Milnes-Voss & Company in 1896. This car was later placed on display at the Home of Rest for Old Horses. (*Kenneth C. Springirth photograph*)

On May 28, 1978, Douglas Bay Horse Tramway open car No. 38 is passing by the beautiful buildings along the promenade in Douglas, Isle of Man. This forty-passenger white with red trim open car was built by G.F. Milnes & Company in 1902. (*Kenneth C. Springirth photograph*)

Seating forty passengers, Douglas Bay Horse Tramway open car No. 42 built in 1905 by G.F. Milnes & Company is on the Douglas promenade with the Irish Sea on the right side on May 28, 1978. This car was rebuilt for the 2017–2018 "Heritage Fleet." (*Kenneth C. Springirth photograph*)

4

Blackpool, England, Trams

The Blackpool Electric Tramway Company (BETC) opened the first tramway in Blackpool, England, on September 29, 1885 as a conduit line (where trams took electricity from a conduit below and in the center of the outside rails) from Cocker Street to Dean Street on the Promenade in Blackpool. When sea water washed into the conduit, it short circuited the traction supply. Sand from beaches blown across the tracks filled up the conduit and with the addition of sea water also short circuited the supply. When the BETC lease expired in 1892, it was taken over by the Blackpool Corporation. In 1899, overhead wiring was installed, the conduit was removed, and in 1900 the line was extended north to Gynn Square where it linked up with Blackpool & Fleetwood Tramroad (B&FT). In 1920, the B&FT was taken over by the Blackpool Corporation.

The last tramway extension was made with the Lytham St. Annes Corporation tramways. In 1936, Routes Central Drive and Layton were converted to bus operation followed by Marton in 1962, and Dickson Road to North Station in 1963. Blackpool Borough Council transferred tram and bus operation to Blackpool Transport Services Limited in 1986.

On February 1, 2008, it was announced that the British Government agreed help fund the upgrading of the tram system. November 6, 2011 marked the last day of running the traditional tram fleet. The entire tram system has been upgraded. On April 4, 2012, the line reopened from Starr Gate in Blackpool in the south to the Ferry Terminus in Fleetwood in the north using the sixteen new Bombardier Flexity 2 trams; some of the "Heritage Fleet" has been retained.

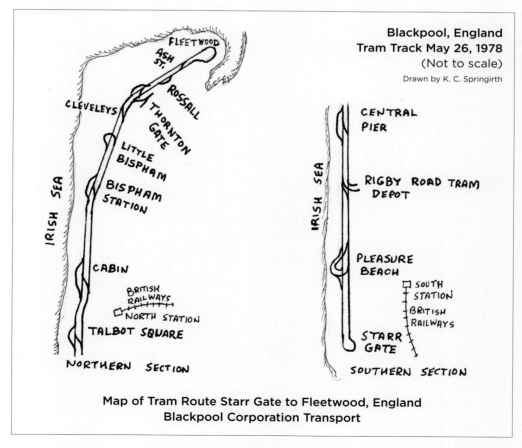

Blackpool, England
Tram Track May 26, 1978
(Not to scale)
Drawn by K. C. Springirth

Map of Tram Route Starr Gate to Fleetwood, England
Blackpool Corporation Transport

The Blackpool Tramway, as shown in the above May 26, 1978 map, connects Starr Gate in Blackpool with Fleetwood on the Fylde Coast in Lancashire, England.

On May 26, 1978, Kenneth Springirth with daughters Grace standing and Kathleen in a baby stroller are admiring Blackpool Tramway tram No. 59 being filmed for a commercial on the Promenade in Blackpool, England. Featuring twin staircases at each end, this double deck open top Dreadnought (named after an English battleship) tram was built in 1902 by the Midland Railway Carriage & Wagon Company. It was out of service from 1935 to 1960, rebuilt by the Blackpool Technical College in 1975, and returned to Blackpool in 1976 for private charters. In 1990, it went to the Crich Museum. (*Virginia M. Springirth photograph*)

On June 4, 1978, Blackpool "Boat" car #600 (one of twelve single-deck open-top trams with central doors originally numbered 225–236 built by English Electric in 1934) is southbound filled with seated passengers on the Promenade in Blackpool stopping to take on more passengers. To the right of the tram is the arrow pointing to the Blackpool train station. In 1968, the eight surviving boat cars were renumbered 600–607. (*Kenneth C. Springirth photograph*)

In a tiger-like paint scheme, Blackpool Brush car No. 622 is at the Rigby Road, Blackpool, England, carbarn waiting for the next assignment on May 23, 1978. Seating forty-eight and having a top speed of 35 miles per hour, the Blackpool Brush cars (Nos. 621–638 [originally Nos. 284–303]) were built in 1937 by Brush Loughborough. (*Kenneth C. Springirth photograph*)

Blackpool tram No. 634, known as a Brush car, is heading southbound for Starr Gate on May 24, 1978. In late 2009, No. 634 was sold to an enthusiast and was returned to Blackpool in 2016 with the car interior restored. (*Kenneth C. Springirth photograph*)

On May 24, 1978, Blackpool Brush car No. 626 in a green and cream paint scheme and rooftop advertising is on the Promenade in Blackpool southbound for Pleasure Beach. A feature of the Brush car, ahead of its time, was driver-controlled air-operated passenger doors. This feature was soon removed when the operator opened the wrong set of doors and some passenger luggage fell out of the tram and was crushed by a passing bus. (*Kenneth C. Springirth photograph*)

Blackpool one-man-operated car No. 2 (originally No. 620, rebuilt in 1972, and later scrapped) is heading for Star Gate on May 24, 1978. This was one of thirteen cars (originally Nos. 608–620 renumbered 1–13; however, the renumbering did not follow the original sequence) built by English Electric and Preston. (*Kenneth C. Springirth photograph*)

On June 4, 1978, many are in line waiting to board Blackpool double-deck Balloon-type tram car No. 703 (originally No. 240) on the Promenade heading for Pleasure Beach. There were twenty-seven of these cars (Nos. 700–727 [originally Nos. 237–263 built in 1933–1935; however, the renumbering did not follow the original sequence). During 1992, most of these cars were changed from trolley pole to pantograph operation. (*Kenneth C. Springirth photograph*)

On a foggy May 27, 1978, Blackpool tram No. 707 on the Promenade is displaying a nice grouping of all over the vehicle advertisements. In 1975, No. 707 was the first Blackpool tram to receive large scale advertising to increase revenues that contributed to keeping the system in operation. The trams were known as Balloon cars because of their streamlined and bloated appearance. Over a period of time, it was recognized that these cars had potential in that they can handle large crowds of riders. (*Kenneth C. Springirth photograph*)

Blackpool tram No. 679 has Manchester Square on its rear roll sign on May 22, 1978. This was originally twin set car No. 279 that was permanently coupled with a trailer car. In 1968, it was converted back to a single tram with a cab at each end; repainted half green, half cream; and became No. 679. (*Kenneth C. Springirth photograph*)

On May 23, 1978, engineering tram No. 7 is on the Promenade in Blackpool. Built in 1924 as passenger car No. 143, it was withdrawn from passenger service in October 1957 and converted into a work car for overhead wire service. It became No. 753 in 1972; however, by 1978 only the No. 7 was visible. (*Kenneth C. Springirth photograph*)

5

Amsterdam, Netherlands, Trams

Amsterdam's first horse-drawn tramway opened on June 3, 1875 by the Amsterdamsche Omnibus Maatschappij (AOM). The Municipality of Amsterdam took over AOM on January 1, 1900 acquiring 242 tramcars and 758 horses under the name Gemeentetram Amsterdam (GTA). By 1906, GTA had twelve electric tram lines and purchased 229 new tramcars. Line 12 (Nassauplein-Sloterdijk)—the last remaining Amsterdam horse tramway—was electrified in 1916. There were twenty-five tram lines by 1931; however, the Great Depression resulted in the abandonment of five tram lintes in 1932: 12, 15, 19, 20, and 21. GTA merged with the Gemeenteveren to form Gemeentelijk Vervoerbedrijf (GVB) on January 1, 1943. During World War II, five lines were suspended, and the entire tram system closed in October 1944 due to a shortage of coal.

Following the end of World War II, tram service was resumed with limited service in June 1945 on lines 1, 3, 5, 7, 9, 10, 12, 13, 16, 24, and 25. Lines 2, 17, and 18 returned in 1947 plus line 4 in 1948. The oldest trams in the system were replaced by sixty trams and fifty trailer cars built by Werkspoor in Utrecht-Zuilen during 1948 to 1950. There was a period in the 1950s when buses were considered to be more practical, and some lines were converted to bus operation. However, by the mid-1950s, modern trams resumed importance. In 1955, twenty-five articulated trams were acquired to serve lines 1 and 2.

Between 1957 and 1968, 160 new articulated trams, built by Beijnes and Werkspoor in the Netherlands were received. The success of these new trams resulted in a decision to replace the Route 17 bus which was serving the suburban community of Osdorp with a Route 17 limited tramline. With Osdorp expected to have an estimated population of 50,000, buses would not have provided adequate service. Construction began on extending the tram line 3 miles from Surinameplein to Osdorp on April 24, 1961 with two miles of track located in the median strip of the Cornelius Leylaan Expressway, and work was completed during August 1962. In rush hours, tram route 17 operated as an express stopping between Surinameplein and Central Station only to discharge passengers inbound and pick up passengers outbound. In October 1971, line 1 was extended to Osdorp. During 1989–1991, forty-five articulated trams (Nos. 817–841 and 901–920) were built by La Brugeoise et Nivelles in Bruges, Belgium. An order was placed for 155 Siemens Combino trams (Nos. 2001–2151 and 2201–2204) which were delivered by mid-2004 replacing the 1960s articulated trams. From 1922 to 1971, each Amsterdam tram had a mailbox

at its rear side which was emptied at Central Station, making it possible to have a letter delivered on time even if it was too late for the last collection from regular mailboxes. The post office's distribution center was located next to the station.

According to the *GVB (Amsterdam Municipal Transport) Facts and Figures for January 1, 1981*, there were 252 dual articulated tram units, eight three-axle tramcars, and eight three-axle trailers which totaled 268 trams. There were 104.3 kilometers of operational double-track tramway of which 53.9 kilometers were on reserved tracks. Average distance between tram stops in the old city 369 meters, areas built in nineteenth century 353 meters, and suburban areas 375 meters. Amsterdam trams operated out of two depots: Havenstraat which opened in 1914 and Lekstraatand which was built between 1927 and 1929.

Rush-hour tram line 6 was introduced on May 27, 2019 between Amsterdam Zuid station and Amstelveen Stadshart; however, because of low ridership, tram line 6 was discontinued on November 6, 2020. Snow storm Darcy caused the shutdown of the entire Amsterdam tram system on February 7, 2021. By February 9, 2021, tram lines 5 and 17 were back in operation. On February 10, 2021, tram lines 1, 3, 4, 13, 14, 24, and 25 still were not running. With motor vehicle traffic pushing snow on the rails and refreezing, it took three days to clear ice and snow on all the tram lines. To help clear the rails, GVB borrowed two preserved work cars and a crew from the Electrische Museumtramijn Amsterdam.

On December 12, 2021 the Amsterdam tramway system had the following fifteen lines:

1: Muiderpoort Station–Weesperplein–Leidseplein–Surinameplein–Lelylann Station–Osdorp De Aker (Matterhorn).

2: Central Station–Leidseplein–Hoofddorpplein–Nieuw Sloten (Oudenaardeplantsoen).

3: Zoutkeetsgracht–Museumplein–Ceintuurbaan–Muiderpoortstation–Flevopark.

4. Central Station–Frederiksplein–Station RAL.

5: Westergasfabriek–Leidseplein–Museumplein–Station-Zuid–Buitenveldert–Amstelveen–Stadshart.

7: Slotermeer–Mercatorplein–Leidseplein–Weesperplein–Alexanderplein–Azartplein.

12: Central Station–Leidseplein–Museumplein–Ceintuurbaan–Amstelstation.

13: Central Station–Rozengracht–Mercatorplein–Geuzenveld (Lambertus Zijlplein).

14: Central Station–Dam–Plantage–Alexanderplein–Flevopark.

17: Central Station–Rozengracht–Kinkerstraat–Lelyaan–Station–Osdorp (Dikgaafplein).

19. Sloterdijk–Leidseplein–Weesperplein–Alexanderplein–Watergraafsmeer–Diemen Sniep.

24: Central Station–Vijzelstraat–Ferdinand Bolstraat–Stadionweg–Amstelveenseweg–VU–De Boelelaan/VU.

25: Station Zuid–Buitenveldert–Amstelveen Westwijk.

26: Central Station–Rietlandpark–Piet Heintunnel–IJburg (Ijburglaan).

27: (Only during the morning peak) Surinameplein–Lelylaan Station-Osdorp (Dijkgraafplein)

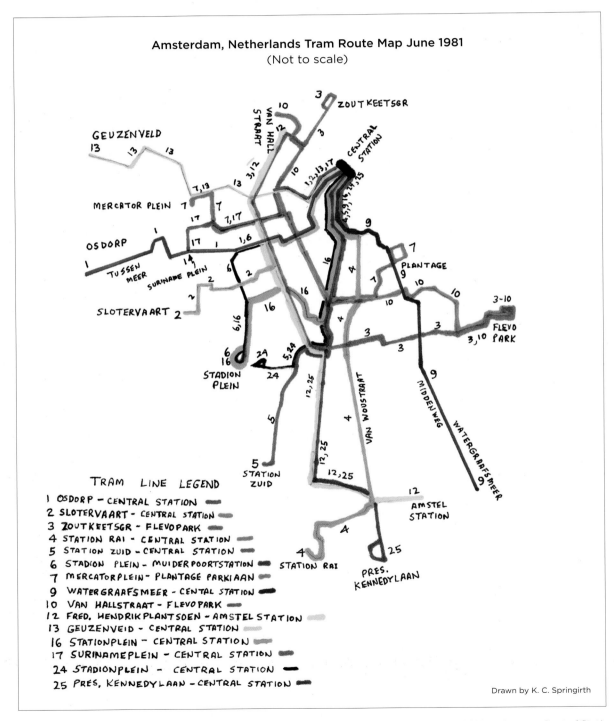

The above map shows that ten of Gemeentetram Amsterdam (GTA)'s fifteen tram lines in June 1981 terminate at Central Station.

On a rainy January 22, 1982, GTA Route 25 tram No. 731 is at the Central Station. This was one of fifty-five articulated type 8G trams (Nos. 725–779) built in 1974–1975 by the German manufacturer Linke-Hoffman-Busch of Salzgitter, Germany. Central Station is the largest railway station in the Netherlands, handling 192,178 daily passengers in 2018. National and international railway service at this station is provided by Nederlandse Spoorwegen (NS), the principal passenger railway operator in the Netherlands. (*Kenneth C. Springirth photograph*)

On January 21, 1982, GTA Route 9 tram No. 802 (type 9G tram one of twenty-five [Nos. 780–804] built by Linke-Hoffman-Busch in 1979–1980) is waiting for departure time at Central Station in downtown Amsterdam. The station, designed by Dutch architect Pierre Cuypers with construction beginning in 1882 by contractor Philipp Holzmann, opened on October 15, 1889. (*Kenneth C. Springirth photograph*)

GTA Route 24 type 9G tram No. 810 (type 10G tram one of twelve [Nos. 805–816] built by Linke-Hoffman-Busch in 1980) is ready to depart on January 21, 1982 from Amsterdam's Central Station with its Gothic/Renaissance Revival architecture characterized by its symmetrical facade and overhanging eves. (*Kenneth C. Springirth photograph*)

On January 21, 1982, GTA type 7G tram No. 707 is at the Route 17 Suriname Plein Loop on January 21, 1982. This was one of twenty-five (Nos. 700–724) built in 1967–1968 by Koninklijke Fabriek van Rijtuigen en Spoorwagens J.J. Beijnes (Beijnes). (*Kenneth C. Springirth photograph*)

6

The Hague, Netherlands, Trams

The Hague is the third largest city in the Netherlands and faces the North Sea. It is only about 13 miles from Rotterdam in an area and economy that relies on an efficient and comprehensive public transit system. On June 23, 1864, the Dutch Tramway Limited opened a horsecar line from city of The Hague, Netherlands, to the nearby resort area of Scheveningen. In 1879, the first steam tram opened in The Hague. The urban tramway company became known as the Haagsche Tramway Maatschappij (HTM) in 1887. Electrification of the system with the use of overhead trolley wire began in August 1904 on a section at the Scheveningen Kurhaus end of Route 9. By 1907, all horsecar lines had been electrified. Improvements to the tram system between 1917 and 1931 included extension of some of the routes into newly built up areas. During World War II, all tram services in The Hague ceased operation on November 17, 1944. Tramway service resumed in The Hague thirty-eight days after the end of World War II on June 11, 1945. Two Presidents' Conference Committee (PCC) cars were ordered in 1948 from St. Louis Car Company in the United States cars and shipped disassembled with final assembly by La Brugeoise et Nivelles at Brugge, Belgium with No. 1001 arriving on July 19, 1949 and soon after by No. 1002. Both cars were well-received by the public and HTM management. They were comfortable, attractive, and had a better acceleration and deceleration than any European tram at that time. An additional order of twenty-two PCC cars (Nos. 1003–1024) were delivered by La Brugeoise et Nivelles at Bruges, Belgium, during 1952 and 1953. PCC cars did require more operating current, necessitating major improvements to the power distribution system plus loops or wyes were needed at each end of the line to allow the use of these single-ended cars. The main differences in the Netherlands version of the PCC car are the use of pantographs for current collection and separate route number indicators. Small windows of the PCC cars were not popular with passengers in The Hague. The next order for PCC cars for The Hague (Nos. 1101–1200) entered service in 1957 had larger windows to please the public plus were designed for multiple unit operation for operational purposes. In 1963, forty additional PCC cars (Nos. 1201–1240) were received with the width of the car increased by 15 centimeters.

Concern about future transportation needs and the need for improvement of transit service resulted in the hiring of Ing F. Lehner, general manager of the Hannover, Germany, tramway system. Lehner's basic recommendation, published on July 15, 1964, was that trams should continue to be the backbone of The Hague transit system noting that a tram track has a higher capacity (in terms of passengers per hour) than a bus lane plus in The Hague 34 percent of the system is on private right of way and to give that up would be a mistake.

On January 4, 1999, new tram Route 17 opened from Central Station to the self-governing community of Rijswijk and peak hour bus route 31 was discontinued. In 2002, new Route 15 opened from Central Station to Nootdorp. In March 2004, a 0.78-mile-long city center tunnel for trams opened with two underground stations Spui and Grote Markt.

In 2017, HTM had three types of trams. The first type GTL8 ("8" stands for eight driven axles with each axle having a Westinghouse PCC DC motor type 1432) is a three-section articulated trams in a red and beige livery. Each was uni-directional with a cab at only one end. These trams were built by La Brugeoise et Nivelles in Bruges, Belgium, with a maximum speed of 70 kilometers per hour and a service speed of 50 kilometers per hours. In the first group were 100 type GTL8-1 (Nos. 3001–3100) series trams (each with a length over buffers of 28.6 meters and weighing 37 tons) delivered during 1981–1984. In the second group were forty-seven type GTL8-II (Nos. 3101–3147) series trams (each with a length over buffers of 29 meters and weighing 38 tons) delivered during 1992–1993. With a width of 2.35 meters and height of 3.19 meters, the GTL8 tram had a maximum speed of 70 kilometers per hour and a service speed of 50 kilometers per hour. On January 2, 2019, No. 3001 (which arrived as the first GTL in The Hague on February 27, 1981) was transported to a recycling company after more than two years out of service.

The second type were seventy-two RegioCitadis bi-directional three section 70 percent low-floor tram-train vehicles in a blue and white paint scheme built by Alstom in Salzgitter, Germany. Fifty-four vehicles (Nos. 4001–4054) entered service in 2006 and eighteen vehicles (Nos. 4055–4072) entered service in 2011. Each vehicle was 36.8 meters long and 2.65 meters wide.

The third type were seventy Avenio, 35-meter-long, 100-percent low-floor trams built by Siemens Mobility in Germany (each having four modules [each supported on its own central bogie] and each accommodating 232 passengers with seventy seated) of which forty were ordered in November 2011, twenty in March 2014, and ten in 2017. Each vehicle end was equipped with a driver's cab for bi-directional operation. Since 2015 the Avenio trams have been gradually replacing the older GTL8 trams. The car body was welded steel construction with extensive use of weatherproof structural steel (Corten) with the entire shell treated with a cathodic dip coating. To facilitate passenger flows, there were one single door plus four double doors arranged on each side over the length of the tram. The driver's cabs and passenger area were air conditioned.

As of 2018, The Hague has twelve tram routes as follows:

1: Scheveningen Noord–Delft Tanthof.

2: Den Haag Kraayenstein–Leidschendam.

3: Den Haag Loosduinen–Zoetermeer Centrum.

4: Den Haag De Uithof–Zoetermeer–Lansingerland–Zoetermeer.

6: Den Haag Leyenburg–Leidschendam Noord.

9: Scheveningen Noorderstrand–VrederuSt.

11: Scheveningen Haven–Den Haag HS Railway Station.

12: Den Haag Duindorp–Den Haag HS Railway Station.

15: Den Haag Central Railway Station–Nootdorp.

16: Den Haag Statenkwartier–Wateringen.

17: Den Haag Central Railway Station–Wateringen.

19: Leidschendam–Delft Railway Station.

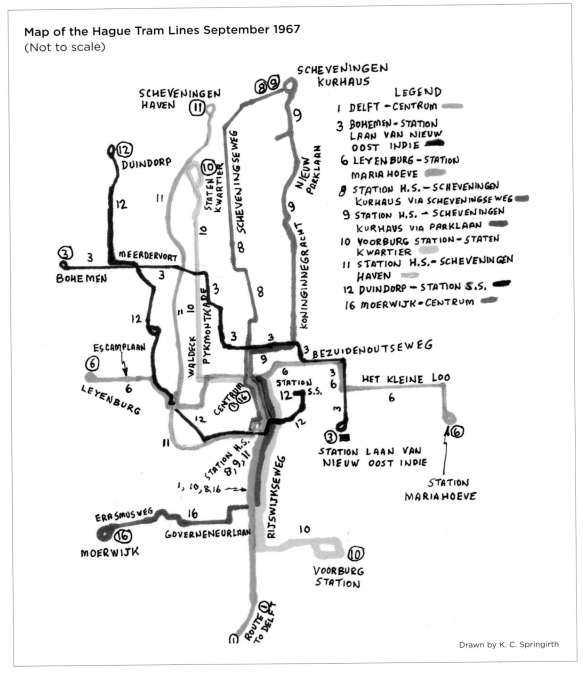

Map of the Hague Tram Lines September 1967
(Not to scale)

Drawn by K. C. Springirth

The above September 1967 map of The Hague, Netherlands, shows nine tram lines. With the rapid growth of nearby satellite suburbs, and Dutch planning regulations requiring that these areas be served by high-quality public transit to avoid more traffic congestion, by 2018 The Hague had twelve tram lines in place.

Haagsche Tramway Maatschappij (HTM) Route 12 President's Conference Committee (PCC) car No. 1101 is handling a trip to Duindorp on January 23, 1982. The first PCC cars No. 1001 and 1002 were two-man operated built in 1949 by La Brugeoise et Nivelles of Bruges, Belgium, using parts received from the United States of America. All future PCC cars ordered by HTM were one-man operated. The first production series (Nos. 1003–1024) were delivered in 1952 still showing their United States ancestry. PCC cars Nos. 1101–1200 had larger side windows. (*Kenneth C. Springirth photograph*)

On January 23, 1982, Laaan Van Merdervoort and Goudenreggen in The Hague is the location of Route 12 HTM PCC car No. 1115 built by La Brugeoise et Nivelles. This car series 1101–1200 with its larger side windows was more European looking. (*Kenneth C. Springirth photograph*)

Waldeck and Van Meedervoort, the junction of Routes 3 and 10, on January 23, 1982 is the location of Route 10 PCC car No. 1211. The arrival of the 1200 class (1201–1240) PCC cars meant the end of the non-PCC car rolling stock. (*Kenneth C. Springirth photograph*)

On January 23, 1982, Route 10 PCC car No. 1217 is heading a two-car train at the Statenkwartier Terminus. Kenneth Springirth, author of this book, is wheeling his young son Peter in a stroller waiting for the doors to open for the next trip. (*Virginia M. Springirth photograph*)

A two-car train of PCC cars headed by PCC car No. 1228 is at the Route 10 Statenkwartier Terminus on January 23, 1982. This was one of forty cars (Nos. 1201–1240) from La Brugeoise et Nivelles. These cars were 15 centimeters wider than the previous 1101–1200 cars, and could run in multiple unit with the 1101–1200 cars, with the wider car leading the train. (*Kenneth C. Springirth photograph*)

On January 23, 1982, two classic trams, Nos. H1 and H9, are ready for their next assignment at the carbarn located on tram route 3 west of the junction with Route 12. (*Kenneth C. Springirth photograph*)

Three section type GTL8-I articulated tram No. 3003 built by La Brugeoise et Nivelles (BN) is at the Route 11 terminus waiting for departure time on January 23, 1982. BN built two different types: GTL8-I Nos. 3001–3100 weighed 37 tons, were 28.6 meters long over buffers, and seated seventy-one. GTL8-II Nos. 3101–3147 weighed 38 tons, were 29 meters long over buffers, and seated seventy-six. These cars were placed in service as follows: 3001–3027 in 1981; 3028–3060 in 1982; 3061–3083 in 1983; 3084–3100 in 1984; 3101–3110 in 1992; and 3111–3147 in 1993. Delivery of this new tram signaled the end of the PCC car era in The Hague. (*Kenneth C. Springirth photograph*)

On January 23, 1982, articulated tram No. 3013 (type GTL8-1 built by BN) is at Van Meerdervoort and Waldeck, the junction of Routes 3 and 10. (*Kenneth C. Springirth photograph*)

7

Rotterdam, Netherlands, Trams

On September 18, 1905, the Rotterdamsche Elektrische Tramweg Maatschappij (RETM) opened Rotterdam's first electric tramline 1 (Honingerdijk–Beurs–Park). RETM was taken over by the municipality of Rotterdam and renamed Rotterdamse Elekrische Tram (RET) on October 15, 1927

On May 10, 1940, service on all lines stopped due to the German invasion, and German bombing destroyed significant areas of Rotterdam. By the end of 1947, the transit system was fully restored from the war damage. On February 9, 1968, a revised Route 2 tram line went into service connecting Charlois with Tuinenhoven. On January 24, 1969, tram Route 5 was extended to Schiebroek. In 2009, Rotterdam had about 118 trams on ten tram routes.

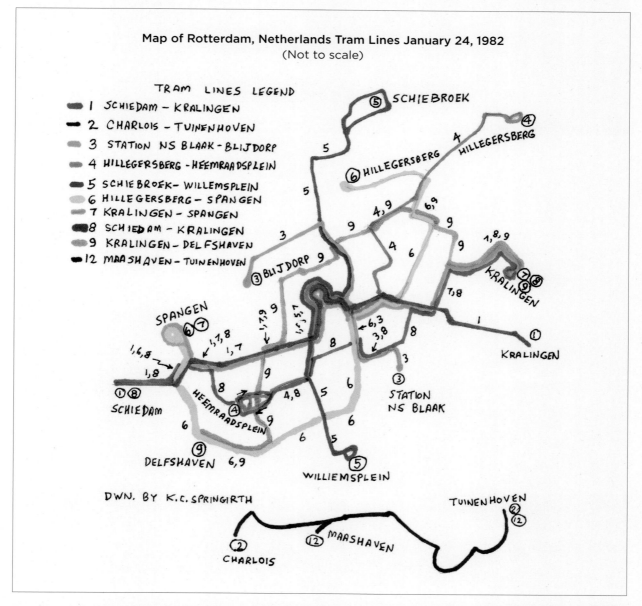

Rotterdamse Elektrische Tram (RET) Rotterdam, Netherlands, had ten tram lines as shown by the above January 24, 1982 map.

On January 24, 1982, RET Route 1 tram No. 319 (one of twenty-four trams [Nos. 301–324] built by Duwag in 1965) in a red and brown paint scheme is at the Route 1 (Schiedam–Koemarkt) terminus. (*Kenneth C. Springirth photograph*)

RET Route 1 tram No. 301, in a green and yellow paint scheme, built by Duwag in 1965 is at Mathenes Serdije on January 24, 1982. (*Kenneth C. Springirth photograph*)

On January 24, 1982, two-section RET type GT6 articulated tram No. 623 (one of thirty-five trams [Nos. 601–635] built by Werkspoor-Duwag in 1968–1969) is on Route 3 at Schiekade near Hoffplein in a zoo tram paint scheme. (*Kenneth C. Springirth photograph*)

Route 5 RET three-section RET type GT8 articulated tram No. 373 (one of thirty-six trams [Nos. 351–386] built in 1964–1965 by Werkspoor-Duwag) is on Weena near Hofplein on January 24, 1982. (*Kenneth C. Springirth photograph*)

On January 24, 1982, Route 7 RET two-section articulated tram No. 237 is at Mathenesserweg. This was one of fourteen trams (Nos. 231–244) built in 1957 by Schindler. (*Kenneth C. Springirth photograph*)

The Route 8 terminus on Kralingen at Chris Bennekerslaan is the location of Route 8 tram No. 320 built by Duewag. (*Kenneth C. Springirth photograph*)

8

Lisbon, Portugal, Trams

On November 17, 1873, the first mule-drawn tramway opened in Lisbon on November 17, 1873 from Santa Apolonia to Santos and was later extended to Belem. In 1888, Companhia Carris de Ferro de Lisboa was granted a ninety-nine-year concession to work an extended network, at the end of which the track and rolling stock would pass to the municipality. Lisbon Electric Tramways was incorporated in London in 1899 to lease the system plus provide the necessary capital and the contract to electrify the system. Praca do Comercio to Alges, the first electric line, opened on August 31, 1901. Suburban routes were added to Carnide, Ajuda, and Areeiro in the 1920s.

In 1957, Lisbon tram routes were as follows: 1: Benfica–Rotunda–Restauradores; 1A: Zoo–Rotunda–Restauradores; 2: Lumiar–Rotunda–Restauradores; 2A: Campo Grande–Rotunda–Restauradores; 3: Bairro Arco do Cego–Anjos–Martim Moniz–Caminho de Ferro; 3A: Campo Pequeno–Rotunda–Restauradores; 3B: Lumiar–Comes Freire–Martim Moniz; 4: Restauradores–S. Sebastiao–Saldanha–Restauradores (circular with Route 5); 5: reverse of Route 4; 6: Praca da Figueira–Martim Moniz–Gomes Freire–Restauradores; 8: Areeiro–Martim Moniz; 9: Poco do Bispo–Praca do Comercio–Cais do Sodre–Santos; 9A: Poco do Bispo–Rua da Alfandega; 10: Graca–Anjos–Martim Moniz–Graca (circular with Route 11); 11: reverse of Route 10; 12: Sao Tome–Martim Moniz; 13: Carnide–Rotunda–Restauradores; 14: Restauradores–S. Sebastiao–Largo do Rato–Restauradores (circular with Route 14A); 14A: reverse of Route 14; 15: Dafundo–Cais do Sodre–Praca do Comercio; 15A: Alges–Cais do Sodre–Praca do Comercio; 15B: Cruz Quebrada–Cais do Sodre–Praca do Comercio; 16: Belem–Conde Barao–Praca do Comercio–Xabregas; 17: Praca do Chile–Martim Moniz–Praca do Comercio–Conde Barao–Belem; 17A: Alto de S. Joao–Praca do Chile–Martim Moniz–Praca do Comercio; 18: Ajuda–Alcantara–Cais do Sodre–Praca do Comercio; 18A: Ajuda–Avenida 24 de Julho–Cais do Sodre–Praca do Comercio; 18B: Boa Hora–Alcantara–Conde Barao–Praca do Comercio; 19: Santo Amaro–Conde Barao–Praca do Comercio–Martim Moniz–Anjos–Arco do Cego; 20: Cais do Sodre–Principe Real–Restauradores–Rossio; 22: Sao Bento–Largo do Rato–Restauradores–Praco do Comercio–Conde Barao–Sao Bento (circular with Route 23); 23: reverse of Route 22; 24: Carmo–Largo do Rato–Campolide–Sao Sebastiao–Praca do Chile; 25: Estrela–Largo do Rato–Restauradores–Praca do Comercio–Conde Barao–Estrela (circular with Route 26); 26: reverse of Route 25; 28: Prazeres–Sao Bento–Rua da Conceicao; 28A: Estrela–Sao Bento–Rua da Conceicao.

In 1958, with the addition of two lines 21 Arco do Cego-Praca do Chile-Alto de S. Joao-Rua da Alfandega and 27 Arco do Cego-Praca do Chile-Alto de S. Joao-Poco do Bispo, Lisbon's tram system had reached its maximum size of about 28 tram lines. During 1958 to 1960, there were 405 motor trams and 100 trailer cars operating on 145 kilometers of track.

In 1959, the company was required modify its tramway and motor bus services because of the opening of the first section of the municipal underground railway. Trams were removed from the Avenida de Liberdade and the Avenida Fontes Pereira de Melo. In 1972, it was announced that trams would be phased out in five years. In 1976, a commission from the Zurich (VBZ) and the Lausanne Transport Institute (ITEP) were invited to report on the Lisbon tramways. The report titled "Lisboa Tramways-Rehabilitation or Substitution" published in August 1978 (that year in which the Lisbon tramway system carried 90 million passenger which represented 19.5 percent of the total Lisbon ridership) recommended the retention and rehabilitation of the tramways in general and of the riverside and lower town routes in particular.

In 1982, Lisbon tram routes were as follows: 3: Arco do Cego–Poco do Bispo; 10: Graca circular (clockwise); 11: Graca circular (counterclockwise); 12: Largo Martin Moniz–Sao Tome; 15: Praca do Comercio–Cruz Quebrada/Estadio; 16: Poco do Bispo–Alges; 17: Alto de Sao Joao–Belem; 18: Praca do Comercio–Ajuda; 19: Arco do Cego–Alcantara; 20: Cais do Sodre–Gomes Freire; 24: Largo do Carmo–Rua da Alfandega; 25: Estrela/Gomes Freire circular (clockwise); 26: Estrela/Gomes Freire circular counterclockwise; 27: Campolide–Poco do Bispo; 28: Graca–Prazeres; 28A: Rua da Conceicao–Prazeres; 29: Estrela/Principe Real circular (clockwise); 30: Estrela/Principe Real circular (counterclockwise). Routes 10, 11, 17, and 20 did not run on Sundays. On Sundays, Route 28 was extended via Graca to Martin Moniz, and Route 19 operates to Alto de S. Joao.

In 2022, Lisbon has five tram lines with E meaning Eletrico which is Portuguese for tram. E12 (Martim Moniz to Martin Moniz) is a one directional clockwise loop. Route E15 (Praca Figueira to Alges) connects Lisbon to Belem using modern articulated trams. E18 (Cais do Sadre to Cemiterio Adjuda) is a quiet route as there are fewer tourist attractions on it. E24 (Praca Luis Camoes to Campolide) connects the Chiado district with the Principe Real district. E25 (Martim Moniz to Campo Ourique) passes through some of the most affluent neighborhoods of Lisbon.

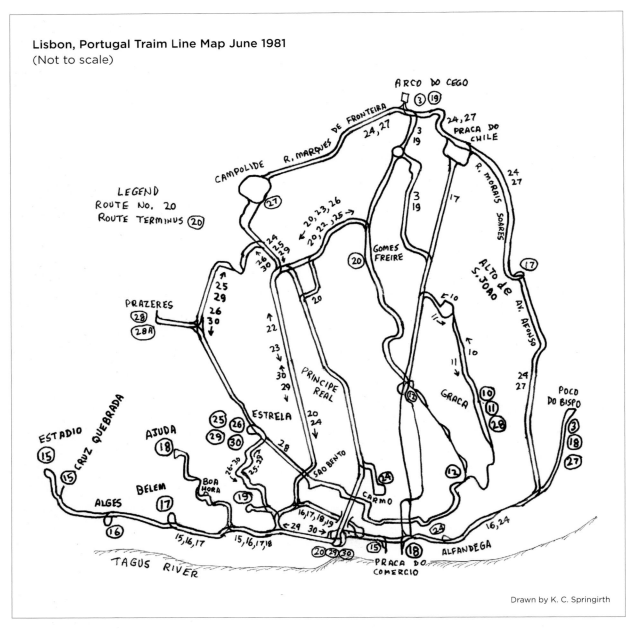

Lisbon, Portugal Traim Line Map June 1981
(Not to scale)

Drawn by K. C. Springirth

The above map shows the following Lisbon tram routes in service in June 1981: 3: Arco do Cego–Poco do Bispo; 10: Graca (circular clockwise); 11: Graca (circular counterclockwise); 12: Largo Martim Moniz–Sao Tome; 15: Praca do Commercio–Cruz Quebrada/ Estadio; 16: Poco do Bispo–Alges; 17: Alto de Sao Joao–Belem; 18: Praca do Comercio–Ajuda; 19: Arco do Cego–Alcantara; 20: Cais do Sodre–Gomes Freire; 24: Largo do Carmo–Rua da Alfandega; 25: Estrela/Gomes Freire (circular clockwise); 26: Estrela/ Gomes Freire (circular counerclockwise); 27: Campolide–Poco do Bispo; 28: Graca–Prazeres; 28A: Rua da Conceicao–Prazeres; 29: Estrela/Principe Real circular (clockwise); and 30: Estrela/Principe Real circular (counterclockwise).

Route 3 Lisbon tram No. 221 is on Avenida Almirante and R. Lozaro in Lisbon, Portugal, on February 24, 1981. The original four-wheel eight-bench open cars (No. 203–282) built by J.G. Brill Company of Philadelphia in 1899 were withdrawn during 1932–1937 with their trucks and motors fitted under new standard bodies. (*Kenneth C. Springirth photograph*)

On February 25, 1981, Route 16 tram No. 293 (one of forty trams [Nos. 283–322] built in 1903 by the J.G. Brill Company of Philadelphia and were replaced by new four wheel trams) is on R. Da Alfandega. (*Kenneth C. Springirth photograph*)

On February 24, 1981, Route 17 tram No. 307 is on Avenida Almirante at R. Lozaro hauling a trailer car at the rear. Driver-controlled air-operated folding doors were only provided at the front of the tram. These cars seated twenty-six passengers and room for twenty-six standees. (*Kenneth C. Springirth photograph*)

Route 3 tram No. 326 is on R. Da Alfandega on February 25, 1981. This was one of twenty trams (No. 323–342) built by J.G. Brill Company in 1906, and all twenty cars were extensively rebuilt and received air brakes during 1931–1932. (*Kenneth C. Springirth photograph*)

On February 25, 1981, Route 15 tram No. 359 (one of twenty trams [Nos. 343–362] built by John Stephenson & Company of New York and delivered in 1906) is at Praca do Comercio in downtown Lisbon for a trip to Cruz Quebrada. These were the first Lisbon trams to have air brakes. (*Kenneth C. Springirth photograph*)

Route 18 tram No. 483, in an advertising paint scheme, is on the Ajuda line on February 25, 1981. This was one of twenty-nine trams (Nos. 475–499 and 503–507) built by J.G. Brill during 1912–1914 and most of these trams received new car bodies during 1952–1963. (*Kenneth C. Springirth photograph*)

Route 10 (Graca) tram No. 490 (in an advertising paint scheme) is being passed by Route 11 (Graca which is the reverse of Route 10) tram No. 432 on February 26, 1981. (*Kenneth C. Springirth photograph*)

On February 26, 1981, Route 17 tram No. 536 (one of twenty trams [Nos. 532–551] built in 1928–1929 with a standard body, domed roof, and vertical sliding windows) is pulling a trailer car. (*Kenneth C. Springirth photograph*)

Route 17 (Belum) tram No. 545 is pulling trailer No. 135 (one of 100 trailer cars [Nos. 101–200] built in 1950–1955 with bus top seats for twenty-eight passengers and standing room for another twenty-eight passengers) along Avenida 24 De Julho at Santos in Lisbon, Portugal, on February 25, 1981. (*Kenneth C. Springirth photograph*)

On February 26, 1981, Route 27 tram No. 555 (one of twenty trams [No. 552–571] built in 1931) is traversing a cobblestone street in Lisbon. (*Kenneth C. Springirth photograph*)

Avenida 24 De Julho at Santos in Lisbon, Portugal, on February 25, 1981, is the location of Route 19 tram No. 613 (one of five trams [Nos. 613–617] built in 1935) followed by tram No. 281 (using the 25-horsepower motors from original cross-bench four-wheel trams that were withdrawn during 1932–1937). (*Kenneth C. Springirth photograph*)

On February 25, 1981, Lisbon Tram No. 801 (one of five trams [Nos. 801–805] built in 1939 with a domed roof, rounded ends, and flush sides) is efficiently handling a Route 19 trip. (*Kenneth C. Springirth photograph*)

9

Porto, Portugal, Trams

A mule-drawn standard-gauge tramway from Porto to Matosinhos opened on May 15, 1872. Another company opened a mule-drawn tramway between Carmo and Foz via Boavista on August 12, 1874. On June 27, 1878, both companies were authorized to use steam traction for their lines. Both companies merged into Companhia Carris de Ferro do Porto (CCFP) on January 18, 1893 and began converting to electric tram operation. Electric service began on September 12, 1895 between Carmo and Rua do Ouro, via Massarelos. Animal traction ended in 1904, and steam traction ended on November 9, 1914. In the mid-1920s, CCFP began building trams using trucks and equipment from the United States. Under the 1906 electrification agreement, the municipality had the option to purchase the system after thirty-five years. After some delay due to World War II, the municipality decided to exercise its option and purchased the CCFP system in 1946 and began municipal operation as Servicio de Transportes Colectivos do Porto (STCP). A circular tram Route 20/21 was constructed, bringing the tram to a maximum route length of 82 kilometers with 150 kilometers of track in 1950 with 191 motor trams and twenty-five trailers carrying 88 million passengers per year. By 1957, trolley buses replaced three tram routes which became trolley bus routes 33, 35, and 36 followed by more conversion to trolley bus operation on May 3, 1959. Following the closure of tram Route 3 (Boavista–Pereiro) on April 30, 1984, the three remaining tram routes were: 1 (Infante–Matosinhos), 18 (Carmo–Castelo do Queijo-Boavista), and 19 (Boavista–Matosinhos). Route 19 and the Matosinhos–Castelo section of Route 1 closed on January 12, 1994, and the remainder of Route 1 closed on September 10, 1994. In 2022, Porto has three heritage tram lines. Route 1 (Passeio Alegre–Infante), Route 18 (Massarelos–Carmo), and Route 22 (Circular Carmo–Batalha).

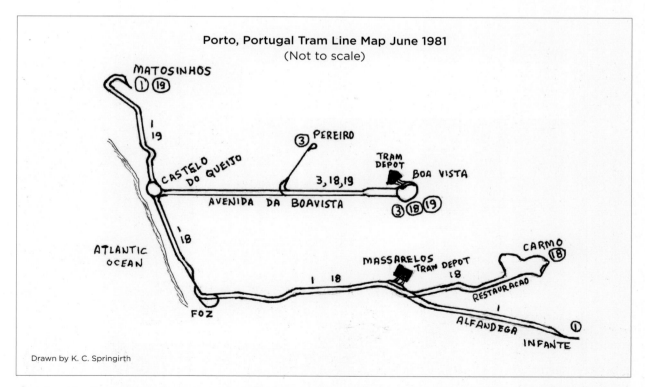

In June 1981, Porto, Portugal had four remaining tram lines 1 (Infante–Matosinhos), 3 (Boavista–Pereiro), 18 (Carmo–Castelo do Queijo-Boavista), and 19 (Boavista–Matosinhos).

On February 28, 1981, Servicio de Transportes Colectivos do Porto (STCP) tram No. 129 (one of seventeen trams [Nos. 120–136] ordered from J.G. Brill of Philadelphia in April 1909) is on Route 18 heading for Carmo. Seating twenty-three passengers, this car had an 18.25-foot-long car body and was powered by two General Electric (GE) type 270 motors. (*Kenneth C. Springirth photograph*)

STCP tram No. 131 is on Route 3 heading for Pereiro on February 28, 1981. The cars of this series were rebuilt to approximately their original design between 1925 and 1938. This car was further rebuilt after 1948 with enclosed platforms having folding doors. (*Kenneth C. Springirth photograph*)

Handling a February 28, 1981 Route 18 trip to Carmo, STCP tram No. 141 was one of ten trams (Nos. 137–146) ordered from J.G. Brill in May 1910 with a 19.33-foot-long tram body that was longer than the 18.25-foot-long body for trams Nos. 120–136. (*Kenneth C. Springirth photograph*)

On February 28, 1981, STCP tram No. 197 is heading for Castelo Do Queijo. The first twenty of the forty trams (Nos. 150–199) were ordered from J.G. Brill in May 1912, and the remainder were built in Porto, Portugal. Tram body length was 19.5 feet. These were the first Porto trams built to a width of 2.40 meters in place of the previous standard 2.25 meters which increased seating capacity to twenty-eight. (*Kenneth C. Springirth photograph*)

Having turned on the circle at Castelo Do Queijo near the Atlantic Ocean on the left, Route 18 STCP tram No. 214 is on Avenida Da Boavista on its way to Boa Vista on February 28, 1981. Seating twenty-eight passengers, this was one of twenty-four trams (Nos. 200–223) seating twenty-eight passengers that were built with Brill 21E trucks by CCFP between 1938 and 1945. (*Kenneth C. Springirth photograph*)

On February 28, 1981, Route 19 STCP tram No. 220 is on Avenida Da Boavista near the Boavista terminus. (*Kenneth C. Springirth photograph*)

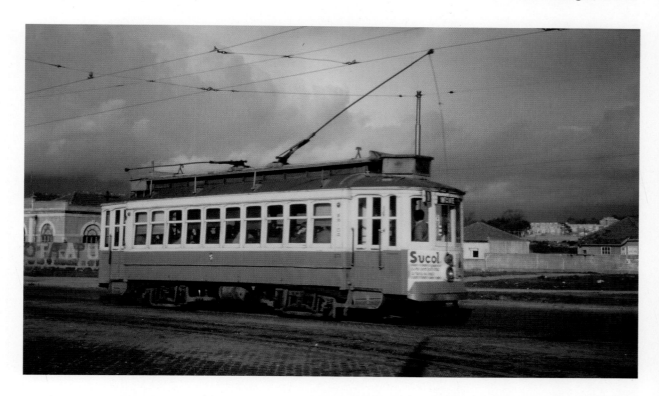

Above: Tram No. 271 (one of eight trams
[Nos. 270–277] built by STCP in 1926–1928 with
bogies [truck assemblies] built by Bergische
Stahl-Industrie of Remscheid, Germany) is
handling a Route 1 trip on February 28, 1981. Seating
forty passengers, the tram length is 11.73 meters,
width is 2.43 meters, and weight is 17.4 tons.
(*Kenneth C. Springirth photograph*)

Right: On March 1, 1978, STCP tram No. 273 is at
the Route 1 Infante Terminus in Porto, Portugal,
where Kenneth C. Springirth, author of this book, is
posing with his young son Peter Springirth. (*Virginia
M. Springirth photograph*)

Under cloudy skies, STCP tram No. 280 is leaving Matosinhos on February 28, 1981 for a Route 1 trip to Infante. This was one of ten trams (No. 280–289) built in 1929 by Ateliers de Construction de Familleureux of Belgium. (*Kenneth C. Springirth photograph*)

On February 28, 1981, STCP tram No. 285 is at Matosinhos waiting for departure time. Despite the heavy look of these trams, they are lighter at 16 tons compared to trams Nos. 270–277 which weigh 17.4 tons. (*Kenneth C. Springirth photograph*)

10

Zurich, Switzerland, Trams

In 1894, the Elektrische Strassenbahn Zurich (EStZ) began electric tram operation in Zurich, Switzerland. The EStZ was taken over by the City of Zurich in 1897 and was renamed Stadische Strassenbahn Zurich (StStZ). In 1927, StStZ introduced its first motor bus route, and in 1939 its first trolleybus route. Crowds were expected to flock to Zurich for the 1939 Swiss National Exhibition which presented a major logistic challenge for Zurich's trams. The objective was to have two prototype trams in traffic during the exhibition. Prototype trams Nos. 31 and 32 operated on six-wheel radially adjusting trucks. Both trams because of their jumping riding qualities became known as a billy goat. A longer third tram, No. 351, arrived (and was renumbered 1351) with state-of-the-art electrical equipment and excellent ride quality. A 1944 conference of public transport operators declared this design the Swiss Standard Tram which after the end of World War II was placed in service in Zurich, Luzern, Bern, Basel, and Geneva. In 1950, StStZ was renamed Verkehrsbetriebe Zurich (VBZ). Tram Route 1 (Burgwies to Hardplatz) was converted to trolleybus Route 31 in 1956 followed by the Farbhof to Schlieren portion of Route 2 to trolleybus in 1958. The trolleybus service struggled to cope with peak loadings and keeping on schedule did not improve.

An example of political leadership was Ruedi Aeschbacher who was elected to the Zurich city executive council from 1978 to 1994. He believed in a non-car-center city. Son of a railway man, he pioneered traffic calming measures putting pedestrians and public transport at the center of his planning rather than cars. Trams have always been popular and well-patronized in Zurich. Public transit improvements in Zurich were achievable politically and financially, because the tram system was still largely intact and well used.

In 1976, the first Tram 2000 (name derived from the numbering series applied to these trams plus reflected modernization of the fleet) entered service with a clean, angular, high-floor design, and large plus clear route indicator display on the front and rear of the tram. In addition to the basic tram (Nos. 2001–2121), a cab-less version (Nos. 2301–2315) was delivered for use with other trams. There was also a shorter non-articulated version (Nos. 2401–2435). During 1976, tram Route 4 was extended from Hardturm to Werdholzli. An initiative was approved by Zurich voters in 1977 to make the existing surface transit system better by providing transit priority for trams and buses. Transit priority means that public transit vehicles are given priority over other forms of transportation by measures such as traffic signal control, transit-only lanes, and traffic regulations. An example is a traffic signal that changes from red to green to favor the tram arriving at the intersection. In the 1990s, the growth of VBZ's operating deficit resulted in lengthening

service frequencies from six minutes to seven minutes and thirty seconds, which reduced the size of the required fleet and permitted withdrawal of some of the older trams. In 1998, Route 11 was extended from Bhf Oerlikon to Messe/Hallenstadion.

After evaluating alternative designs, in 2001, VBZ took delivery of six Cobra type (five section units with a length of 36 meters) trams (Nos. 3001–3006) which featured a large surface of glass to separate the operator's cab from the passenger area to improve security, and to enhance reading there were halogen spots mounted above the seats. The new design was initially plagued by excessive noise and vibrations plus problems with doors and gearboxes. After the problems were corrected, VBZ ordered sixty-eight units (Nos. 3007–3074).

Zurich's blue and white trams serve most of Zurich's neighborhoods with most tram routes running from city periphery to city periphery via the city center plus not only transporting large number of passengers, but also are an integral part of the city's identity. Trams are chartered for theatre performances and for readings. Zurich does not permit allover vehicle advertising. However, a maximum of three tram sets may be repainted to provide educational information such as informing the public about alternative energy or wild animals in the city. Instead of a rolling billboard, theme trams can enhance the travelling experience. A Zurich without trams would probably be a city with more automobiles, more concrete, and less quality of life. A September 25, 2003 Statistik Stadt Zurich study noted that of the 125,000 people who both live and work in the city of Zurich, 65 percent travel to and from work by public transit, 17 percent use a car, 10 percent a bicycle, and 6 percent walk all the way. In a March 3, 2003, study by Mercer Human Resource Consulting (London) comparing standards of living in 215 cities of the world based on thirty-nine criteria reflecting political, social, and economic factors, Zurich had the highest standard of living. Zurich shows that people want trams, and that trams are good for cities.

The Forchbahn opened on November 27, 1912 from the Zurich city boundary to Esslingen. In 1970, a new depot was built at Forch. New Tram 2000 trains were placed in service along with a fifteen-minute service frequency in 1976. Between the Stadelhofen Railway Station in Zurich to Rehalp, Forchbahn trains use VBZ tram tracks which are electrified at 600 volts DC. Rehalp is the terminus of VBZ Route 11, and the Forchbahn is electrified at 1,200 volts on its own double-track alignment past Rehalp. Past Waltikon Station, the Forchbahn enters a double-track tunnel with underground stations at Zumikon and Maiacher. In 1970, the line was single track beyond Neue Forch Station to its terminal point at Esslingen.

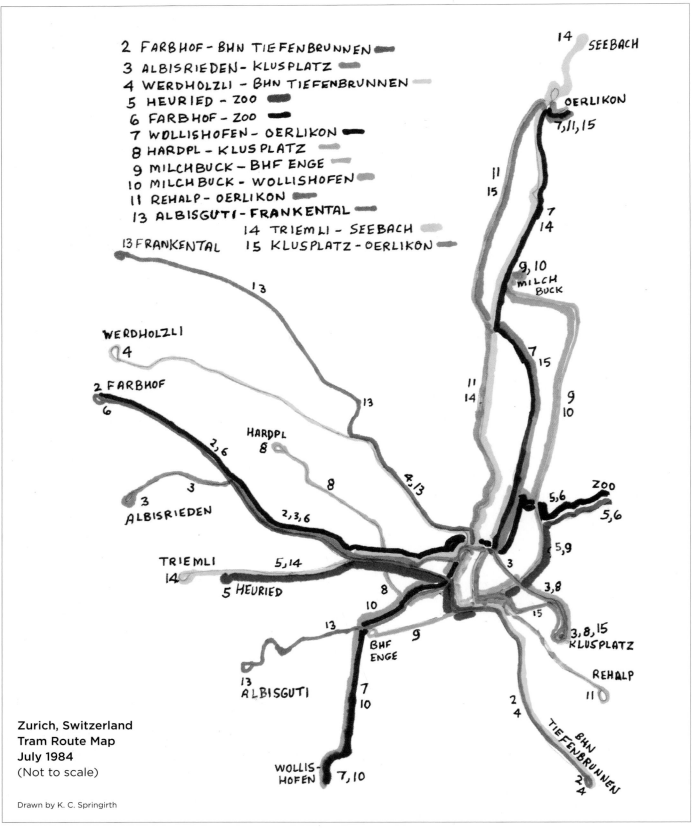

2 FARBHOF – BHN TIEFENBRUNNEN
3 ALBISRIEDEN – KLUSPLATZ
4 WERDHOLZLI – BHN TIEFENBRUNNEN
5 HEURIED – ZOO
6 FARBHOF – ZOO
7 WOLLISHOFEN – OERLIKON
8 HARDPL – KLUSPLATZ
9 MILCHBUCK – BHF ENGE
10 MILCHBUCK – WOLLISHOFEN
11 REHALP – OERLIKON
13 ALBISGUTI – FRANKENTAL
14 TRIEMLI – SEEBACH
15 KLUSPLATZ – OERLIKON

Zurich, Switzerland
Tram Route Map
July 1984
(Not to scale)

Drawn by K. C. Springirth

The above map shows, in July 1984, the tram system makes an important contribution to public transportation in Zurich, Switzerland, because the density and interconnectedness of Zurich's tram system has made it convenient to travel to almost any point in the city contributing to making Zurich one of the most livable cities in the world.

On July 17, 1984 in Zurich, Switzerland, Route 2 (heading for Tiefenbrunnen) tram No. 1605 is one of ninety type ZM6s trams (Nos. 1601–1690) built in 1966–1968 by Schweizerische Waggons und Aufzugefabrik AG, Schlieren (SWS)/Schweizerische Industrie-Gesellschaft (SIG). (*Kenneth C. Springirth photograph*)

Route 3 tram No. 1684 type ZM6s built in 1966–1968 by SWS/SIG is at a passenger stop bound for KlutsPlatz on July 18, 1984. (*Kenneth C. Springirth photograph*)

With parallel overhead trackless trolley wire on the left, Route 3 tram No. 1689 type ZM6s built in 1966–1968 by SWS/SIG is at a pedestrian crossing on July 18, 1984. (*Kenneth C. Springirth photograph*)

On July 17, 1984, Route 4 (heading for Tiefenbrunnen) type M4s tram No. 1547 is one of thirty-four trams (Nos. 1519–1552) built in 1949–1952 by SWS. (*Kenneth C. Springirth photograph*)

In this July 18, 1984 scene, "Goldtimer" vintage tram No. 1016 is a historic 1928 vintage tram taking Zurich residents and their guests on delightful trips past historic buildings and city landmarks in Zurich. The completely restored tram was painted gold, and its May 2–October 14, 1984 timetable showed it operated on Wednesday, Friday, and Sunday departing at 10:30 a.m., 11:30 a.m., 2:15 p.m., and 3:30 p.m. from the Globus-"Goldtimer-Terminal." (*Kenneth C. Springirth photograph*)

Route 6 tram type M4S No. 1387 built by SWS with No. 726 type B4S built by SIG are loading passengers in Zurich on July 17, 1984. (*Kenneth C. Springirth photograph*)

On July 17, 1984, Forchbahn trams Nos. 27 and 28—five twin-car sets with two numbers per set, making a total of ten trams (Nos. 21–30)—(Tram 2000 design [a high-floor design for the Verkehrsbetriebe Zurich first introduced in 1976] built during 1976–1981 by SWS) are at the Rehalp terminus of VBZ Route 11. Beyond this point the Forchbahn provides suburban tram service to Esslingen. (*Kenneth C. Springirth photograph*)

In this July 17, 1984 scene, Forchbahn tram No. 107 is one of seven trams (Nos. 102–108) built by Schweizerische Waggons und Aufzugefabrik AG, Schlieren (SWS)/Schindler Waggon AG, Pratteln (SWP) during 1967–1968. Once a rural tramway, the Forchbahn was threatened with conversion to bus operation in the 1950s; however, it has survived to become a very successful light rail transit line. (*Kenneth C. Springirth photograph*)

On a sunny July 18, 1984 day in Zurich, Route 10 tram No. 1379 type M4s built by SWS with a trailer car behind it is heading for Milchbuck. (*Kenneth C. Springirth photograph*)

Route 10 tram No. 1389 type M4s built by SWS is making a southbound run on July 18, 1984 for Wollishofen. (*Kenneth C. Springirth photograph*)

In downtown Zurich on July 18, 1984, Route 10 tram No. 1426 type, one of fifteen trams (Nos. 1416–1430) built by Schweizerische Waggons und Aufzugefabrik AG, Schlieren (SWS), is in a lineup of trams. (*Kenneth C. Springirth photograph*)

In a pleasant, well-maintained Zurich commercial center, Route 11 tram No. 1624 (built by SWS/SIG) with a trailer car behind it is carefully making its way for a southbound trip to Rehalp on July 17, 1984. (*Kenneth C. Springirth photograph*)

On July 17, 1984, Route 11 tram No. 1802 (type JM6s built in 1960 by SWS) is southbound for Rehalp. (*Kenneth C. Springirth photograph*)

Heading to Rehalp on July 17, 1984 is well-designed type "Tram 2000" No. 2019, one of forty-five trams (Nos. 2001–2045) built during 1976–1978 by Schweizerische Wagons und Aufzugefabrik Schlieren (SWS)/Schindler Waggon AG, Prattein (SWP). (*Kenneth C. Springirth photograph*)

On July 18, 1984, downtown Zurich is the location of Route 13 type ZM6s tram No. 1678 built by SWS/SIG on a trip to Frankental. (*Kenneth C. Springirth photograph*)

On a sunny July 17, 1984, Route 15 type M4s tram No. 1524 is traversing a somewhat winding paved roadway. (*Kenneth C. Springirth photograph*)

11

Basel, Switzerland, Trams

The first Basel, Switzerland, tram line opened on May 6, 1895 from the Basel central railway station to the Basel Baden railway station. In 1900, a new cross-border tram line was opened to St. Louis, France. During World War I and II, tram service was suspended on the parts of any tramline extending beyond Switzerland's borders. Tram service from Basel to St. Louis, France, ended in 1950. Tram service operated from Basel to Huningue, France, from 1910–1961. Tram service operated from Basel to Lorrach, Germany, from 1919–1967. On December 14, 2014, Basel tram line 8 was extended 1.7 miles to Weil am Rhein, Germany. Basel tram line 3 was opened to St. Louis, France, on December 10, 2017 with four stops in France. Basel is connected by tram to both Germany and France making it the only tram system in the world operating trams in three different countries. The other tramway systems in the world crossing an international border are Route 17 of Transport Public Genevois just after Moillesulaz Station in Geneva, Switzerland, to Annemasse-Parc-Montessuit Station in France which opened on December 15, 2019, and line D of the Strasbourg Tramway from Strasburg, France, via Port du Rhil, France, to Kehl Rathous Station in Kehl, Germany, which opened on April 28, 2017. Basel's location, services, and visual charm make it a popular destination. As of 2022, Basel's trams have been in existence for 127 years, making it part of Basel's heritage and a symbol of the city.

Basel trams are operated by two systems: Basler Verkehrs-Betriebe Basel Transport Service (BVB) and Baselland Transport (BLT). BVB is owned by the small canton consisting of the city of Basel and two smaller communities. Its green trams operate predominately in the city of Basel; however, lines 3, 6, and 14 have their terminals in the more rural canton of Basel-Land. BLT (formed on January 1, 1974 by merging Birsigtalbahn [BTB], Birseckbahn [BEB], and Basel-Aesh tramway (TBA) to form Baselland Transport AG (BLT) Basel-Land operating yellow and red trams in the outer suburbs south of Basel. Its three lines 10, 11, and 17 also run over BVB track in central Basel. It should be noted that the 15.9-mile Line 10 runs from Basel, Switzerland, crossing into France with a station at Leymen, France, and crossing back into Switzerland to serve Rodersdorf, Switzerland. For customs purposes, trams operate through France as privileged transit traffic. Passengers staying on the tram are not subject to customs rules. Passengers may get on or off the tram only if they are carrying goods within the customs limits. In addition, while line 14 is owned by BLT, it is operated by BVB into Basel-Land.

On July 28, 1984, Basel Verkehrs-Betriebe (BVB) Route 6 tram car No. 624 (one of fifty-five type JM6s tram cars [Nos. 603–658] built by Duewag during 1967–1973) has on the front destination sign Riehen Grenze which is close to the German border. (*Kenneth C. Springirth photograph*)

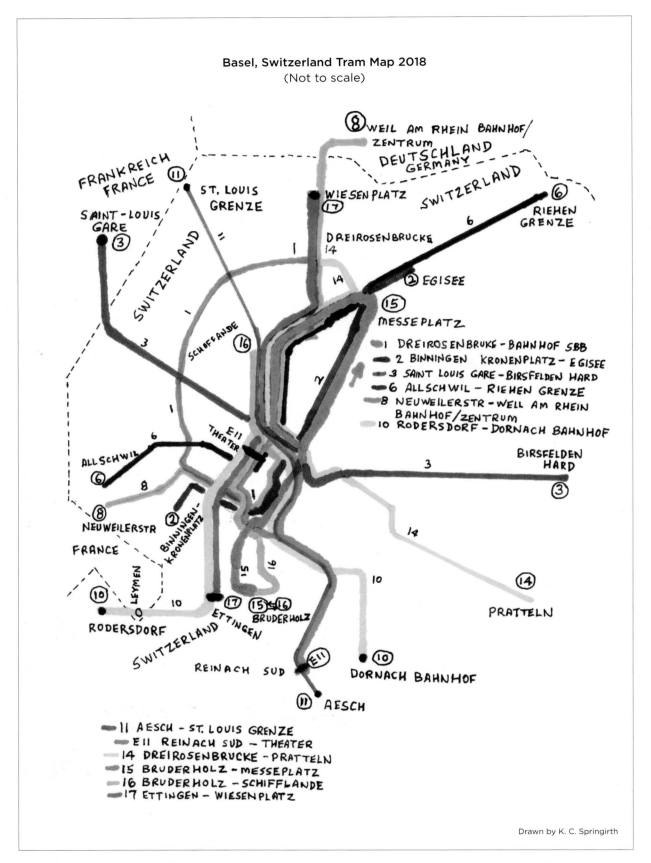

Basel, Switzerland Tram Map 2018
(Not to scale)

1 DREIROSENBRUKE - BAHNHOF SBB
2 BINNINGEN KRONENPLATZ - EGISEE
3 SAINT LOUIS GARE - BIRSFELDEN HARD
6 ALLSCHWIL - RIEHEN GRENZE
8 NEUWEILERSTR - WELL AM RHEIN BAHNHOF/ZENTRUM
10 RODERSDORF - DORNACH BAHNHOF

11 AESCH - ST. LOUIS GRENZE
E11 REINACH SUD - THEATER
14 DREIROSENBRUCKE - PRATTELN
15 BRUDERHOLZ - MESSEPLATZ
16 BRUDERHOLZ - SCHIFFLANDE
17 ETTINGEN - WIESENPLATZ

Drawn by K. C. Springirth

Basel, Switzerland, on the border of France and Germany, has a comprehensive tram system as shown in the above map. In 2018, BVB operates tram routes 1, 2, 3, 6, 8, 14, 15, and 16 while BLT operates tram routes 10, 11, and 17.

On July 28, 1984, Route 6 Duewag built tram No. 625 (one of thirty-six trams [Nos. 623–658] built by Duewag during 1972–1973) in its pleasing malachite green with white stripe paint scheme, is coming into a passenger stop in Basel, Switzerland, with a waiting group of passengers ready to board on the line that terminates close to the German border. (*Kenneth C. Springirth photograph*)

Baselland Transport (BLT) tram No. 109, in a magnificent chrome yellow with broad red stripe paint scheme, is handling a Route 10 trip to Dornach on July 28, 1984. This was one of fifteen type JM6s trams (Nos. 101–115) built in 1971–1976 by Schindler Wagon AG, Prattein (SWP). (*Kenneth C. Springirth photograph*)

On July 28, 1984, BLT type JM6s tram No. 112 is waiting for departure time for a Route 10 trip to Dornach. (*Kenneth C. Springirth photograph*)

Here is a striking contrast on July 28. 1984 between BLT trams Route 10 tram No. 113 built by SWP in 1976 and Route 11 tram No. 226 one of sixty-six trams (Nos. 201–266) built by SWP in 1978–1981. (*Kenneth C. Springirth photograph*)

In downtown Basel, Switzerland, BVB Route 16 tram No. 470 (one of seventy-six type M4s trams [Nos. 401–476] built by SWP) is passing BVD Route 14 tram No. 1490 (one of ninety-one type B4s trams [Nos. 1416–1506] built by Flug und Fahrzeugwerke AG/Schindler Waggon AG, Prattein in 1961–1972) on July 28, 1984. (*Kenneth C. Springirth photograph*)

On July 28, 1984, BVB Route 16 tram No. 461, built by SWP, is heading south to Bruderholz. (*Kenneth C. Springirth photograph*)

BLT Route 17 type cB4d tram No. 23 (one of seven [Nos. 21–27] built in 1966 by Schweizerische Waggons und Aufzugefabrik AG, Schlieren [SWS]) is in downtown Basel on July 28, 1984. (*Kenneth C. Springirth photograph*)

On July 28, 1984, BLT tram No. 21 built by SWS is operating over a private right of way section interurban line that would today be known as a light rail line. (*Kenneth C. Springirth photograph*)

12

Bern, Switzerland, Trams

On July 18, 1889, the Bernese Tramway Company (BTG) was granted an eighty-year concession for the operation of trams in Bern, and the first line, I, opened on October 1, 1890 from Barengraben to Bremgartenfriedhof. Service was provided by compressed air-powered lufttrams (air trams). In the winter months, the compressed air pipes sometimes froze, resulting in service interruptions which resulted in city residents voting to have steam trams operate line II which opened from Langgasse to Wabern. Voters approved that line III would be electric operated which opened on July 1, 1901 from Breitenrain to Burgernziel. Line IV opened on June 27, 1908 from the railway station to Bruckfeld. On November 18, 1923, a branch line was opened from Effingerstrasse to Fischermatteli. In 1947, the Stadtische Strassenbahn Bern (SSB), which operated trams and trolley buses, merged with the Stadt-Omnibus Bern (SOB), which operated motor buses, to form the

Stadtische Verkehrsbetriebe Bern (SVB), the public transport operator in and around the city of Bern which is also known by its marketing name Bernmobil. While Bern had a population of about 136,000, in 2009 SVB transported 89.4 million of which 30.7 million were carried by tram. At the end of the 1990s, a transit study recommended that certain existing bus and trolley bus service be converted to tram operation by 2020. On June 17, 2007, voters of the canton of Bern approved the investment credit needed for that conversion. Construction work began on April 1, 2008 for the tram line extension beginning at a junction at Kaufmannischer Verband and proceeding to Bumpliz underpass where the line divides into tram Route 7 to Bumpliz and tram Route 8 to Brennen. The extended tram service opened on December 12, 2010 at which time tram Route G to Worb was renamed Route 6 and extended to Fischermatteli.

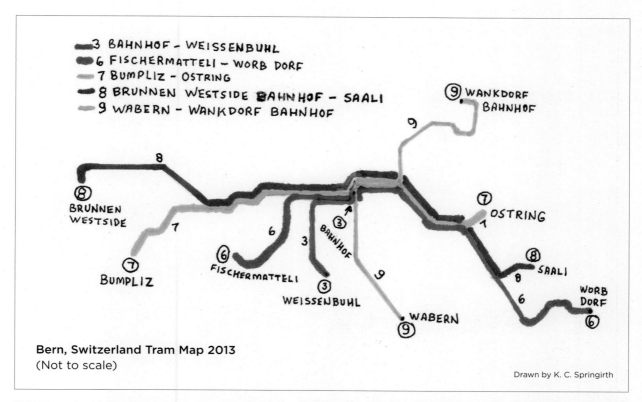

Bern, Switzerland Tram Map 2013
(Not to scale)

Drawn by K. C. Springirth

As of 2013, the above map shows the Bern, Switzerland, tram lines which operate on a 3-foot 3.375-inch gauge track as follows: 3: Bahnhof–Weissenbuhl, 2.067 kilometers long; 6: Fischermatteli–Worb Dorf, 13.067 kilometers long; 7: Bumpliz–Ostring, 8.109 kilometers long; 8: Brunnen Westside Bahnhof–Saali, 10.383 kilometers long; and 9: Wabern–Wankdorf Bahnhof, 5.958 kilometers long.

SVB tram No. 104 (one of fifteen type M4s trams [Nos. 101–115] built in 1947–1948 by Schweizerische Waggons und Aufzugefabrik AG, Schlieren (SWS) is on the Route 3 private right of way heading for Weissenbuhl on July 26, 1984. (*Kenneth C. Springirth photograph*)

On July 26, 1984, downtown Bern, Switzerland, is the location of Route 3 tram No. 125 (one of ten trams [Nos. 121–130] built in 1960–1961 by SWS) with the destination sign indicating a trip to Weissenbuhl. (*Kenneth C. Springirth photograph*)

In the late afternoon of July 26, 1984, Bern, Switzerland, Route 5 tram No. 109 (one of fifteen type M4S trams [Nos. 101–115] built in 1947–1948 by SWS) with a trailer car behind it, is handling a trip to Fischermatteli. Since 1984, the number of tram lines in Bern has increased, and in 2013 Route 6 connected Fischermatteli with Worb Dorf. (*Kenneth C. Springirth photograph*)

On July 26, 1984, Route 9 tram No. 8 (one of sixteen type JM8S trams [Nos. 1–16] built by SWS in 1973) is heading for Wabern. (*Kenneth C. Springirth photograph*)

Under an overcast July 26, 1984 sky, Bern, Switzerland, Route 9 tram No. 15 (built by SWS in 1973) has just pulled away from a passenger boarding island for a trip to Wabern. (*Kenneth C. Springirth photograph*)

Downtown Bern, Switzerland, is the location of Route 9 tram No. 16 (built by SWS in 1973) headed for Wabern on July 26, 1984. (*Kenneth C. Springirth photograph*)

13

Geneva, Switzerland, Trams

The first horse-drawn tramway in Geneva, Switzerland, opened on June 19, 1862 connecting Place de Neuve with Rondeau. That section is today served by electric tram Route 12. Geneva's first electric tramway opened in 1894. Compagnie Genevoise des Tramways Electriques (CGTE), formed in 1899, bought out the other companies, electrified all the lines, and established a uniform meter gauge. Economic problems and cheaper bus alternatives in 1925 resulted in the CGTE beginning to convert its interurban lines to bus operation. In the city of Geneva, lines were converted to bus and partly by trolley bus. By 1969, only Route 12 (Moillesulaz–Carouge which had been in existence since 1862) remained with the good condition of the tram cars contributing to the retention of the line. Formed in 1977, Transport Public Genevois (TPG) in 1995 constructed a one-mile extension across the Rhone River to Cornavin, Geneva's main railway station.

In 1987–1989, TPG obtained forty-five new, partly low-floor articulated trams based on the prototype tram No. 741, which had been added to the TPG fleet in 1984. The new trams were built by Ateliers de Constructions Mecaniques de Vevey (ACMV) in collaboration with Duewag and BBB/ABB.

Route 15 (Palettes–Nation) opened in 2003. Route 14 (Bernex Vailly–Meyrin–Graviere) opened in 2007. In 2006, approval was given to construct a line mainly in the center of the Route de Meyrin traffic artery to CERN (the research site of the European Organization for Nuclear Research) which opened as Route 18 (Palettes CERN) in 2012. Route 17 Lancy Pont–Rouge Gare was extended almost 2 kilometers on December 15, 2019 into France to Annemasse–Parc–Montessuit. Up until the 1950s, Geneva had a tram line to Annemasse; however, the wide-scale abandonments resulted in only Route 12 surviving by 1969. Geneva now has a tram network of five lines.

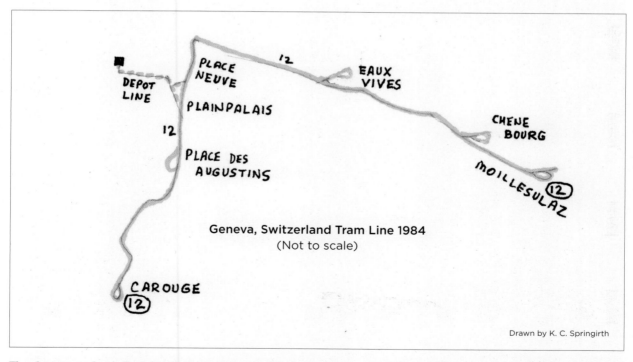

Geneva, Switzerland Tram Line 1984
(Not to scale)

Drawn by K. C. Springirth

The above map shows the 5.6-mile Route 18 line in 1984 before the one-mile extension to Cornavin, Geneva's main railway extension that signaled a new future for Geneva's trams.

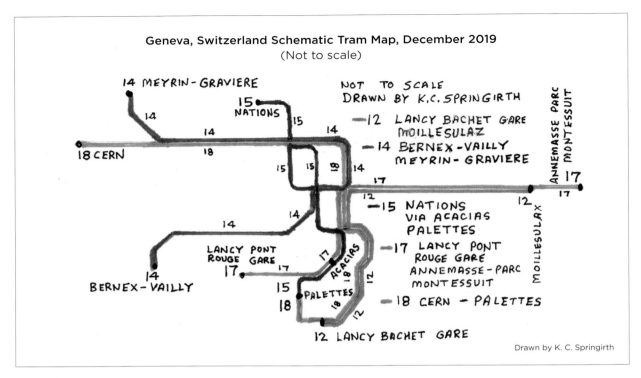

Geneva, Switzerland Schematic Tram Map, December 2019
(Not to scale)

As a result of the rebirth of Geneva's trams, since 2019, the tram system, as shown by the above map, had the following lines:
12: Lancy–Bachet–Gare Moillesulaz; 14: Bernex–Vailly Meyrin–Graviere; 15: Nations via Acacias–Palettes; 17: Lancy–Pont Rouge
Gare–Annemasse–Parc Montessuit); and 18: Palettes CERN.

On July 28, 1984, Transport Public Genevois (TPG) tram No. 717 (one of thirty trams [Nos. 701–730] built by Schindler Waggon
AG, Pratteln (SWP) during 1950–1952) is heading for Carouge. (*Kenneth C. Springirth photograph*)

On July 28, 1984 on display in Geneva at the museum siding and owned by the L'Association Genevoise du Musee des Tramways (AGMT) are trams No. 67 type M4d built in 1901 by Herbrand (CGTE) and rebuilt in 1939 plus tram No. 363 type B4d built in 1920 by Schweizerische Industrie-Gesellschaft (SIG). (*Kenneth C. Springirth photograph*)

On a cloudy July 28, 1984, Route 12 tram No. 724 (one of thirty trams [Nos. 701–730] built by SWP during 1950–1952) is handling a trip to Carouge. (*Kenneth C. Springirth photograph*)

Route 12 tram No. 712, built by SWP, is making a passenger stop at Place de Neuve, meaning new place, which is one of the main squares in Geneva on July 28, 1984. (*Kenneth C. Springirth photograph*)

The Rivo passenger stop in Geneva is the location of Route 12 tram No. 741 on July 28, 1984. This was a new prototype tram type SM6s built in 1984 by Ateliers de constructions mecaniques, Vevey (ACMV)/Duewag. (*Kenneth C. Springirth photograph*)

14

Neuchatel, Switzerland, Trams

The Regional Neuchatel-Boudry Cortaillod (NCB) steam interurban tramway including an Areuse–Cortaillod branch line opened on September 16, 1893. The first urban tramway, Tramway Neuchatel–St. Blaise (NSB) opened powered by gas on September 16, 1893; however, problems with gas-engined vehicles resulted in the line being converted into a horsecar line. This line was electrified in 1897. During 1898, the Port–Gare line opened followed by three more lines: Place Pury–Serrieres in 1899; Place Pury–Vauseyon in 1901; and Peseux–Corcelles in 1902. During 1901, NSB merged with NCB to form Compagnie des Tramways de Neuchatel. By 1926, there were six urban tram routes 1, 2, 3, 4, 6, and 7 in operation. Between 1940 and 1976, the urban tram routes were converted to trolley bus routes. First to close was Route 2 to Serrieres in 1940 followed by Route 4 to Valangin in 1949, Route 1 to Blaise in 1957, Routes 6 and 7

to Neuchatel Railway Station in 1964, and Route 3 from Place Pury to Corcelles was the final urban tram line to close on July 11, 1976. The interurban line from Boudry to Pl. Pury remained in service.

On December 31, 1982, the interurban line had fourteen cars as follows: Nos. 501–504, built in 1981 by Schweizerische Waggons und Aufzugefabrik AG, Schlieren (SWS); Nos. 551–554 built in 1981 by Schweizerische Waggons und Aufzugefabrik AG, Schlieren (SWS); Nos. 581–583 built in 1947 by Schweizerische Industrie-Gesellschaft (SIG); and Nos. 592–594 built in 1942. The Compagnie des Transports en commun de Neuchatel et environs (TN) was the public transport operator in and around the Swiss city of Neuchatel operating the city's network of trams, trolley buses, and motor buses, under the marketing name Transports Publics du Littoral Neuchatelois. It merged with Transport Regionaux Neuchatelois in 2012 to form the Transports Publics Neuchatelois.

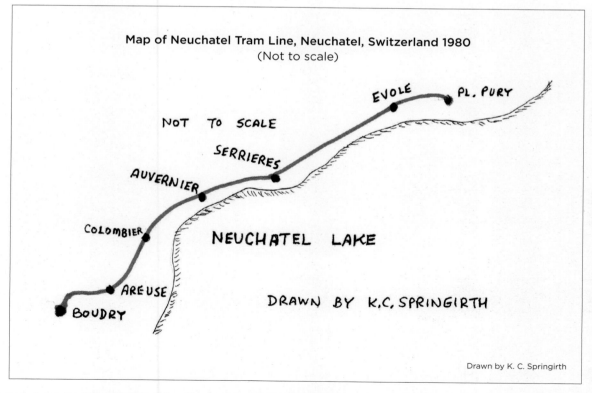

Map of Neuchatel Tram Line, Neuchatel, Switzerland 1980
(Not to scale)

NOT TO SCALE

EVOLE   PL. PURY

SERRIERES

AUVERNIER

COLOMBIER

NEUCHATEL LAKE

AREUSE

BOUDRY

DRAWN BY K.C. SPRINGIRTH

Drawn by K. C. Springirth

The above map shows the 5.9-mile interurban line connecting Boudry with Place Pury which is about 0.6 miles from the Neuchatel train station. In the early 1980s, this line was completely relaid, realigned, fitted with automatic block signals, and equipped with new rolling stock.

On July 26, 1984, the author's wife Virginia Springirth with their children Grace, Peter, and Philip along with another passenger are waiting to board one of the Neuchatel trams that had been delivered in 1981 in an attractive color scheme of yellow with green around the windows. Trams Nos. 501–504 seated forty-two passengers with standing room for sixty-five passengers. Trams Nos. 551–554 seated forty-six passengers with standing room for sixty-seven passengers. All of these trams were built by SWS in 1981. (*Kenneth C. Springirth photograph*)

Neuchatel tram No. 501 with a Route 5 with a Route 1 (Marin) trolley bus along with other public transit vehicles in the distance behind it on July 26, 1984 provides an example of a well-designed transit system. Public transit ridership in Neuchatel increased from 2.46 million passengers in 1978 to 3 million in 1980. That is an impressive figure with Neuchatel having a population of 32,819 in 2009. (*Kenneth C. Springirth photograph*)

At Auvernier station in the municipality of Milvignes in the Swiss canton of Neuchatel on July 26, 1984, passengers are preparing to board tram No. 501 for Neuchatel while Tram No. 553 is waiting for departure time for Boudry. A Swiss canton (of which there are twenty-six cantons in Switzerland) oversees everything from schools and police forces to health care and taxes. It is almost like a state in the United States. (*Kenneth C. Springirth photograph*)

On July 26, 1984, from left to right, the author's children Peter, Kathy, Grace, with Philip in stroller, and wife Virginia Springirth are by a Neuchatel tram with its basic characteristics as follows: maximum speed 75 kilometers per hour, car body length 17,480 millimeters, car body width 2,400 millimeters, car body height 3,173 millimeters, and wheel diameter 660 millimeters. A millimeter is .03937 inches. (*Kenneth C. Springirth photograph*)

In this July 26, 1984 scene, Neuchatel control trailer tram No. 553 is one of four (Nos. 551–554) built in 1981. While a motor tram has a driving position at both ends, a control trailer tram has a driving position at only one end. This provides flexibility of train formation from a single motor tram to two motor trams plus two control trailers in multiple unit formation. (*Kenneth C. Springirth photograph*)

Neuchatel No. 501 is traversing a scenic portion of Route 5 on this single track interurban line connecting Boudry with Place Pury on July 26, 1984. At one time Route 5 was predicted to close; however, local authorities came to appreciate the merits of the line with its efficient private right of way operation which in 2022 would be known as a light rail line. (*Kenneth C. Springirth photograph*)

15

Helsinki, Finland, Trams

In June 1891, a horse-drawn tram line was opened by Helsinginraitiotie ja omnibussiosakeyhtio (abbreviated HRO). In 1897, HRO received approval to construct an electric tram line in Helsinki. The contract was awarded to O.L. Kummer of Germany to construct the system, provide the trams, and operate it for up to three years to make sure the system was acceptable. HRO took over the successful new electrified four single-track tram route network in 1901. In a few years, the single-track lines became unable to meet passenger demand; however, the majority of stockholders were unwilling to fund the conversion into double track. In 1906, Julius Tallberg and his associates acquired a majority of HRO stock, and applied for permission to double track the tram system which was received in 1906. Swedish ASEA was awarded the contract to double track the network which began in 1908 and was completed in 1910. Between 1908 and 1919, ASEA supplied HRO with seventy-eight trams and seventy trailers.

The city of Helsinki acquired the majority of HRO stock in 1913; however, HRO remained an independent company. In 1914, the tram network was extended into Taka-Toolo and Hermanni. The tram network reached its peak in 1930 with fourteen lines in operation.

At the end of 1944, the City of Helsinki acquired HRO, making it a municipal transit authority named Helsingin Kaupungin Liikennelaitos (HKL). During the 1950s, 105 Finnish-built trams were delivered to HKL. Trams remained the main public transport until the 1960s with private automobiles more common, and the new suburbs mainly served by buses and commuter trains. In 1969, Helsinki City Council decided that in the future tram lines would be confined to the inner city, the metro would serve the suburban areas, and the tram system would end at the earliest in the year 2000.

The decision to end the tram system was reversed and in 1976, the tram network was expanded for the first time since 1955 when the new connection into Ita-Pasila opened (then Route 2, present Route 7). In 1980, tracks in Katajanokka were extended eastward to a new residential area (then Route 5, present Route 4). In 1985, the tram system was extended to West Pasila (Route 7). In the mid-1980s, there were numerous minor and to major changes. Next expansion of the system occurred in 1991 when the connection from Ruskeasuo to Pikku Huopalahti opened. In 2004, Route 6 was extended from Arabia to Arabianranta. A new Route 9 opened on August 10, 2008 connecting Kolmikulma in central Helsinki to East Pasila which was the first new tram line in Helsinki since the opening of Route 2 in 1976.

On a sunny July 18, 1985, in Helsinki, Karia HM V class tram No. 9 is at a passenger stop on Route 1A. This was one of fifteen trams (Nos. 1–15) delivered in 1959, built by the Finnish tram manufacturer Karia. These were the last trams built by Karia, and were also the last four-axle tram class to be delivered for service in Helsinki. (*Kenneth C. Springirth photograph*)

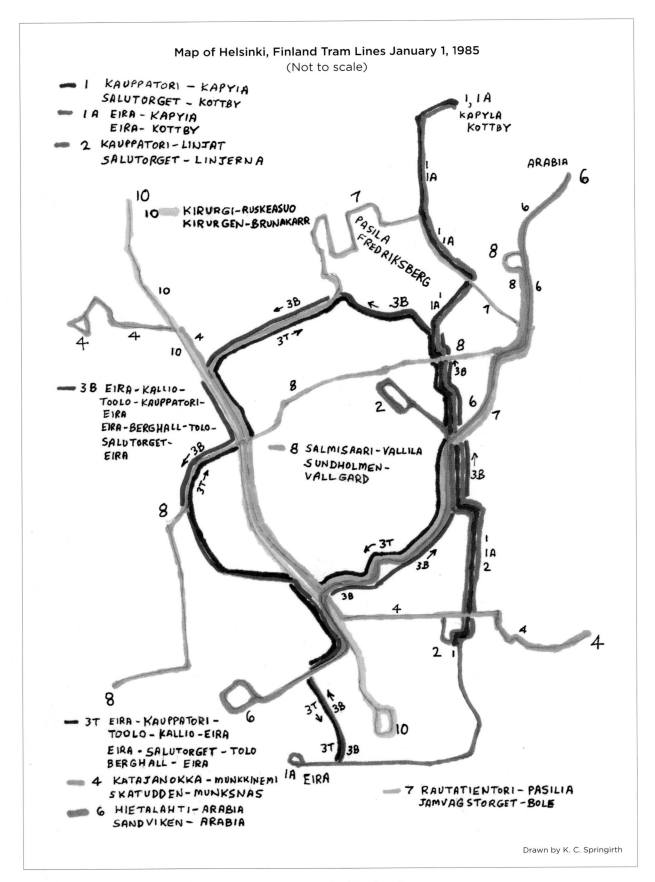

Map of Helsinki, Finland Tram Lines January 1, 1985
(Not to scale)

1   KAUPPATORI – KAPYIA
    SALUTORGET – KOTTBY
1A EIRA – KAPYIA
    EIRA – KOTTBY
2   KAUPPATORI – LINJAT
    SALUTORGET – LINJERNA

10 KIRURGI – RUSKEASUO
    KIRURGEN – BRUNAKARR

3B EIRA – KALLIO –
    TOOLO – KAUPPATORI –
    EIRA
    EIRA – BERGHALL – TOLO –
    SALUTORGET –
    EIRA

8   SALMISAARI – VALLILA
    SUNDHOLMEN –
    VALLGARD

3T EIRA – KAUPPATORI –
    TOOLO – KALLIO – EIRA
    EIRA – SALUTORGET – TOLO
    BERGHALL – EIRA
4   KATAJANOKKA – MUNKKINEMI
    SKATUDDEN – MUNKSNAS
6   HIETALAHTI – ARABIA
    SANDVIKEN – ARABIA

7   RAUTATIENTORI – PASILIA
    JAMVAGSTORGET – BOLE

Drawn by K. C. Springirth

The above January 1, 1985 map shows the ten tram lines in Helsinki at that time.

On July 20, 1985, Route 6 Helsinki tram No. 367 is in downtown Helsinki. This was one of forty-five Valmet RM I class trams (Nos. 331–375) delivered during 1955–1956 and remained in regular service until the mid-1980s when it was replaced by the new Nr II class. (*Kenneth C. Springirth photograph*)

Route 3T Helsinki tram No. 64 is at a passenger stop in Helsinki on July 19, 1985. This was one of forty trams type Nr I (Nos. 31–70) (first type of articulated tram operated by HKL) built by Valmet in Tampere, Finland, between 1973 and 1975. The design of the Nr I trams was based on the German Duewag GT6 type built starting in 1956. From November 1993 to July 2004, all Nr I trams were modernized by HKL including the addition of electronic display displaying the name of the next stop and installing new seats. (*Kenneth C. Springirth photograph*)

On July 20, 1985, Helsinki tram No. 72 is handling a Route 7 trip. This was an Nr II class tram, one of forty-two (Nos. 71–112) built by Valmet between 1983 and 1987. Between 1996 and 2005, all of the Nr II trams were modernized by HKL and re-designated as Nr II+. (*Kenneth C. Springirth photograph*)

Helsinki tram No. 73 is on a private right of way section of Route 7 on July 20, 1985. Between 2006 and 2011, all Nr II class trams were rebuilt with a low-floor midsection and redesignated MLNRV II. (*Kenneth C. Springirth photograph*)

16

Melbourne, Australia, Trams

Melbourne, Australia, has the largest tramway system in the English-speaking world. It began as a horse-car line from the Fairfield railway station to a real estate development in Thornbury that opened on December 20, 1884 and closed by 1890. On November 11, 1885, the Melbourne Tramway & Omnibus Company (MT&OC) opened Melbourne's first cable car line operating from Bourke Street to Hawthorn Bridge via Spencer Street, Flinders Street, Wellington Parade, and Bridge Street. At its peak, Melbourne's cable car system operated 1,200 cable cars (grip cars and trailers) on seventeen routes covering 64.12 route miles.

Melbourne's first electric tramway opened in 1889 from the Box Hill train station to Doncaster; however, disputes and operational problems resulted in closure in 1896. Victorian Railways opened an electric street railway from St. Kilda railway station to Middle Brighton on May 5, 1906 and was extended to Brighton Beach on December 22, 1906. The Melbourne & Metropolitan Tramways Board (MMTB) was formed in July 1919 and took over Melbourne's cable tram network, six of the seven electric tramway companies, and the last horse tram. By 1940, all cable and horse tram lines were abandoned or converted to either electric tram or bus operation.

After World War II, many cities around the world replaced their trams with buses. However, Melbourne replaced Bourke Street buses with trams in 1955, and new tram lines opened to East Preston and Brunswick East. Melbourne did not shut down the tram network for the following reasons: Melbourne's wide streets and geometric street pattern made trams more practicable than in many other cities; resistance from the unions; MMTB Chairman Sir Robert Risson, noted that the cost of ripping up the concrete-embedded tram tracks would be prohibitive; and the infrastructure and trams were relatively new which countered the argument used in other cities that renewal of the tram system would cost more than replacing it with buses. Even with the decline in ridership beginning in the 1950s due to the increasing use of automobiles and population shift to the outer suburbs beyond the trams network limits, Melbourne retained its trams. In 1978, tram service was extended along the Burwood Highway. The W-class trams were gradually replaced by the new Z-class trams in the 1970s and by the A-class trams and larger articulated B-class trams in the 1980s. On July 1, 1983, the MMTB was absorbed into the newly formed Metropolitan Transit Authority (MTA). By April 11, 1988, rail, tram, and bus divisions were fully integrated into the MTA. The St. Kilda

and Port Melbourne railway lines were converted to light rail lines in 1987 which consisted of re-gauging the track from broad gauge 5 feet 3 inches to standard gauge 4 feet 8.5 inches, overhead wires converted to tramway voltage, and light rail platforms built adjacent to the former station platforms. Regional rail assets were merged into the State Transit Authority (STA) on July 1, 1983. Under the Transport (Amendment) Act of 1989, the MTA and STA were merged into the Public Transport Corporation (PTC) on July 1, 1989 bringing all rail services in Victoria under one body. With the need to reduce the costs of operating Melbourne's public transport system, tram conductors were replaced by ticketing machines between 1996 and 1998. As part of a privatization process effective November 30, 2009, Keolis Downer (joint venture between Keolis and Downer EDI) became the operator of the Melbourne tram system. The existing tram fleet has been refurbished, fifty-nine new Siemens Combino (D-class) low-floor trams were acquired from Siemens, and thirty-nine Alstom Citadis (C-class) low-floor trams were acquired. Extensions to the tram system have been made with Route 109 extended to Box Hill on May 2, 2003 and Route 75 to Vermont South on July 23, 2005.

Comeng built 100 new Z1-class trams between 1975 and 1979. The Z1-class tram made its last run on April 23. 2016. There were fifteen Z2-class trams built between 1979 and 1984. The Z2-class tram made its last run on April 21, 2016. Between 1979 and 1984, 115 Z3-class trams entered service. Comeng built twenty-eight A1-class trams, built with trolley poles, between 1984 and 1985 followed by forty-two A2-class trams, equipped with pantographs, between 1985 and 1986. B2-class trams, the first Melbourne trams with air conditioning, entered service between 1988 and 1994. The first 130 were built by Comeng and later ABB. In 2001, thirty-six three-section, articulated, low-floor C-class vehicles manufactured in France by Alstom were placed in service. During 2002 to 2004, German made Siemens Combino trams were obtained, and as of April 25, 2020, thirty-seven (three-section D1-class) and twenty (five-section D2-class) trams were available for service. Bombardier Transportation's Dandenong, Australia built fifty three-section, articulated E1-class trams with the first placed into service on November 4, 2013 and the last on April 24, 2017. Melbourne's tram ridership has increased from 129.4 million for the July 1, 2000 to June 30, 2001 period to 206.3 million for the July 1, 2017 to June 30, 2018 period.

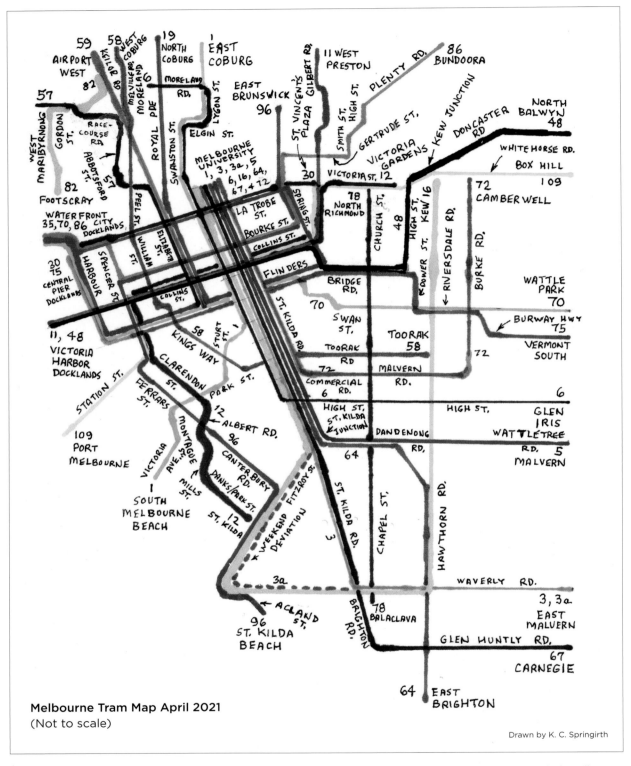

Melbourne Tram Map April 2021
(Not to scale)

Drawn by K. C. Springirth

This map shows Melbourne's twenty-four full-time tram routes as follows: 1: East Coburg–South Melbourne Beach; 3: Melbourne University–East Malvern; 5: Melbourne University–Malvern; 6: Moreland–Glen Iris; 11: West Preston–Victoria Harbor Docklands; 12: Victoria Gardens–St. Kilda; 16: Melbourne–Kew; 19: North Colburg–Flinders Street Station; 30: St. Vincent's Plaza–Central Pier Docklands; 35: City Circle; 48: North Balwyn–Victoria Harbour Docklands; 57: West Maribyrnong–Flinders Street Station; 58: West Colburg–Toorak; 59: Airport West–Flinders Street Station; 64: Melbourne University–East Brighton; 67: Melbourne University–Carnegie; 70: Wattle Park–Waterfront City Docklands; 72: Melbourne University–Camberwell; 75: Vermont South–Central Pier Docklands; 78: North Richmond–Balaclava; 82: Moonee Ponds–Footscray; 86: Bundoora RMIT–Waterfront City Docklands; 96: East Brunswick–St Kilda Beach; and 109: Box Hill–Port Melbourne.

On May 16, 1977, L-class tram No. 105 was chartered by Kenneth Springirth, the author of this book. This was one of a class of six trams (Nos. 101–106) ordered by the Prahran & Malvern Tramways Trust (PMTT); however, by the time they were delivered in 1921, the PMTT was taken over by the Melbourne & Metropolitan Tramways Board (MMTB). In 1934, this car series was modified with two wider doors replacing the four narrow doors. These cars were withdrawn from regular service in 1969. (*Kenneth C. Springirth photograph*)

MMTB W2-class tram No. 381 is handling a Route 5 trip on St. Kilda Road on May 16, 1971. There were 200 W-class trams (Nos. 219–418) built during 1923–1927 by Holden, James Moore & Sons, and MMTB. Between 1925 and 1928, all 200 were converted to W2 class between 1928 and 1933. The 406 W2-class trams became the backbone of the MMTB fleet from the 1940s to the 1960s. (*Kenneth C. Springirth photograph*)

On a rainy May 24, 1977, W2-class tram No. 558 is at the Melville Road and Bell Street terminus of Route 56. The W2-class tram had a drop center section in the middle of the tram and had wooden bench-style seats. While there were variations in the types of gears on W2-class trams, W2-class trams with spur gears were notable because of their humming sound. (*Kenneth C. Springirth photograph*)

Hawthorne and Balaclava is the location of MMTB Route 64 W2-class tram No. 633 on May 18, 1977. This intersection has a grand union where there are two double tracks crossing at grade with sixteen switches in place to allow a tram to go straight or make a right or left turn from any approach track. Melbourne has the only surviving grand union on a tram line in the southern hemisphere. (*Kenneth C. Springirth photograph*)

On May 24, 1977, Route 20 MMTB W5-class tram No. 770 is on Flinders and Elizabeth Street in downtown Melbourne There were 120 W5-class trams (Nos. 720–839) built by the MMTB from 1935 to 1939. Many of the W5-class trams were allocated to Essendon and Brunswick depots. (*Kenneth C. Springirth photograph*)

A rainy May 24, 1977 finds W5-class tram No. 827 at Melville Road and Bell Street with the front destination sign showing Essingdon Depot. With the exception of those severely damaged in accidents, the first W5-class tram was withdrawn in 1987 and the last in 1994. By January 2020, there were no SW5 and no W5 trams remaining in service. (*Kenneth C. Springirth photograph*)

The Route 49 Matthews Avenue and Niddrie terminus finds type SW6 tram No. 871 waiting for departure time on May 23, 1977. There were 120 type SW6 trams (Nos. 850–969) built by MMTB during 1939 to 1951. An improvement over earlier designs was the installation of sliding doors in the center section which kept the tram warmer in winter. (*Kenneth C. Springirth photograph*)

Swanston and Victoria is the location of Route 5 type SW6 tram No. 888 on May 17, 1977. The longevity of the W-class trams was due to the excellent engineering of their original design which achieved a reliable, high-capacity, and effective rail transit vehicle. (*Kenneth C. Springirth photograph*)

On May 23, 1977, MMTB Route 59 type SW6 tram No. 910 is at Mt. Alexander and Keilor. Seating fifty-two passengers, the tram was 14.17 meters long, 2.73 meters wide, and had a wheel diameter of 711 millimeters. San Francisco's Market Street Railway operates two Melbourne trams: SW6-class No. 916 (entered service in Melbourne on June 21, 1946) and W2-class No. 496 (went into service in Melbourne on February 18, 1928). (*Kenneth C. Springirth photograph*)

Victoria and Gisborne finds MMTB Route 12 tram No. 984 heading to downtown Melbourne on May 18, 1977. This was one of thirty type W6-class trams (Nos. 970–979 and 981–1000) built during 1951–1955. (*Kenneth C. Springirth photograph*)

On Elizabeth Street in downtown Melbourne, Route 57 tram No. 1001 (one of forty W7-class trams [Nos. 1001–1040] built in 1955–1956 by MMTB) is passing Route 52 tram No. 283 (one of 200 W-class trams [Nos. 219–418] built in 1923–1927 by Holden, James Moore & Sons and MMTB). The W7-class trams had upholstered seats but otherwise were very similar to the preceding W6-class trams. (*Kenneth C. Springirth photograph*)

Route 81 W7-class tram No. 1005 is behind another MMTB tram on Elizabeth Street at Flinders Street in downtown Melbourne with the historic Edwardian-style (characterized by its prominent dome flanked on each by a smaller cupola, arched entrance, and red brick with yellow pressed cement decoration) Flinders Street train station behind the trams on May 17, 1977. The forty W-class 7 trams were originally built for the new Bourke Street tram service that replaced bus service on June 26, 1955. (*Kenneth C. Springirth photograph*)

On May 17, 1977, MMTB W7-class tram No. 1024 is at the Riverdale Road and Elgar Route 70 terminus in a unique colorful eye catching advertising paint scheme. (*Kenneth C. Springirth photograph*)

Route 11 W7-class tram No. 1036 is handling a trip to West Preston on May 16, 1971. (*Kenneth C. Springirth photograph*)

On May 16, 1977, Z1-class tram No. 22 is handling a Route 96 trip. Construction of the new trams started at Comeng Dandenong in 1974 with the first tram entering service on Route 64 on May 5, 1975 and the second new tram on Route 72 on May 7, 1975. As more of the new trams were delivered, the first fifteen were kept at North Fitzroy Depot to operate on Route 96 beginning on June 30, 1975. (*Kenneth C. Springirth photograph*)

Route 96 Z1-class tram No. 53 is on Park Street passing the North Fitzroy Depot on May 18, 1977. Shortly after being placed in service, it was noted that the new Z1-class tram had ride problems due to stiff suspension and track differences between where they were built and Melbourne. The issues were resolved by the time the eightieth new tram was built by means of rubber secondary suspension that was retrofitted to all of the new trams. (*Kenneth C. Springirth photograph*)

17

Adelaide, Australia, Trams

In 1873, a 5-foot 3-inch steam railroad was built from downtown Adelaide to Glenelg. Adelaide's first horse tram was completed from downtown Adelaide to Kensington and North Adelaide in May 1878. The Adelaide-Glenelg line was transferred to the Municipal Transport Trust (MTT) in 1927, rebuilt to standard gauge 4 feet 8.5 inches, and was converted to tramway operation, reopening in late 1929. A trolleybus system was established in 1937 and remained in service until July 1963. Motor buses replaced trolley buses. On July 12, 1963, the Glenelg line was the only surviving tram line. During 2005–2006, the Glenelg line received a $22 million upgrade which included rebuilding 6 miles of track plus improved electrical and signal systems. A 0.75-mile extension opened in August 2007 extending the Glenelg line along King William Street and west along North Terrace through the Adelaide

railway station and the western city campus of the University of South Australia. By September 2006, nine new Bombardier Flexity Classic trams arrived. Two new additional Flexity Classic trams arrived in 2007 for the extension which opened on October 14, 2007. During 2015, all of the original type H Glenelg trams were out of service. By December 2017, nine Citadis model 302 trams manufactured by Alstrom originally for the Metro Ligero in Madrid arrived. An extension was completed in 2010 from the existing North Terrace terminus to the Adelaide Entertainment Center. An eastward extension to Botanic Gardens opened on October 13, 2018. Following a July 2019 government announcement that tram services and other Adelaide transport services would be contracted out, in July 2020, Torrens Connect began operating Adelaide trams under an eight-year contract.

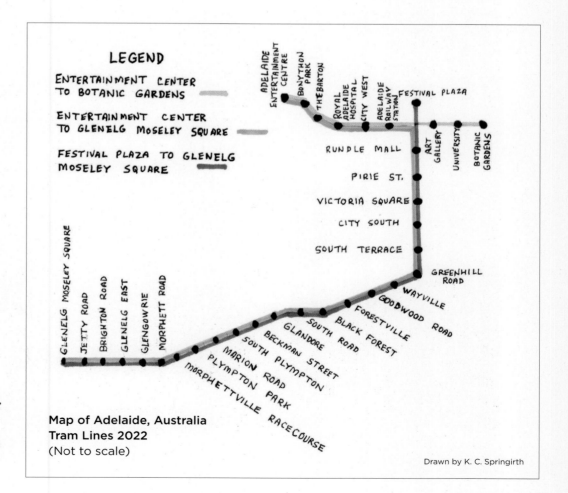

This 2022 map of the Adelaide, Australia, tram system shows the extension to the Adelaide Entertainment Centre and the extension serving the Botanic Gardens.

Map of Adelaide, Australia Tram Lines 2022
(Not to scale)

Drawn by K. C. Springirth

On May 20, 1977, tram No. 372 is one of two type H trams (in a Tuscan red and cream paint scheme) parked across the street from the Adelaide, Australia, tram depot. The thirty type H trams (Nos. 351–380) were built in 1929 by the A. Pengelly & Company located on South Road in Edwardstown located 6 kilometers southwest of Adelaide. (*Kenneth C. Springirth photograph*)

Type H tram No. 379 is one of two trams in the silver and carnation paint scheme (used during 1952–1956) parked in front of the Adelaide tram depot on May 20, 1977. (*Kenneth C. Springirth photograph*)

Adelaide type H tram car No. 364 along with another type H tram on May 20, 1977 are waiting for departure time at the Adelaide tram depot. Both trams have a resemblance to North American streetcars. (*Kenneth C. Springirth photograph*)

A two-car train of type H trams with No. 375 in the lead are at Tram Stop 11 (Plympton Park 36 Lindsay St.) heading back to downtown Adelaide on May 20, 1977. Plympton Park is an inner south-western suburb of Adelaide about 8 kilometers from the central business district of Adelaide. (*Kenneth C. Springirth photograph*)

Type H tram No. 357 is passing the Morphettville Racecourse on May 19, 1977, for major horseracing, in Morphettville, a suburban area about 10 kilometers from the city center of Adelaide. The racecourse is directly opposite the Stop 12 Morphett Road tram station. The suburb and racecourse were named after Sir John Morphett, a landowner and member of the legislative council who took an interest in horseracing in South Australia. (*Kenneth C. Springirth photograph*)

On May 19, 1977, type H tram No. 363 is passing one of the local stops on the Glenelg tram line. (*Kenneth C. Springirth photograph*)

Type H tram No. 358 is at on Jetty Road in Glenelg, a beachside suburb of the Southwestern capital of Adelaide, on May 19, 1977. Moseley Square (a public square named for Henry J. Moseley who was a noted builder in Glenelg) is the terminus of the Glenelg tram line. (*Kenneth C. Springirth photograph*)

Jetty Road at Sussex Street in Glenelg is the location of type H tram No. 368 on May 19, 1977. Established in 1836, Glenelg was named for Lord Glenelg, a member of the British cabinet and secretary of state for war and the colonies. (*Kenneth C. Springirth photograph*)

On May 20, 1977, left of tram No. 369, which is on Jetty Road near Glenelg Beach at Moseley Square, is the 36-foot-high Centenary Monument that was erected and unveiled on December 28, 1936 to commemorate the landing of British pioneer settlers 100 years earlier. Looking at the top of the monument is a bronze model of the HMS *Buffalo* (originally built in 1813 as the merchant vessel *Hindostan*, acquired later in 1813 by the British Royal Navy for shipping naval supplies, became a convict ship in 1833, transported immigrants to Australia in 1836, and was wrecked in Mercury Bay at New Zealand in 1840). (*Kenneth C. Springirth photograph*)

Package in hand a passenger is approaching tram No. 367 on Jetty Road at the end of the line near Glenelg Beach for the return trip to Adelaide on May 20, 1977. (*Kenneth C. Springirth photograph*)

18

Hong Kong Trams

Tracklaying began in May 1903 on the 3-foot 6-inch gauge line of the Electric Traction Company of Hong Kong Limited line from Kennedy Town to Shaukiwan with a branch line to Happy Valley. On July 2, 1904, the first car, No. 16, left the depot and operated on the Happy Valley branch and a portion of the main line. The line officially opened at 10 a.m. on July 30, 1904. During 1910, the company name changed to Hong Kong Tramway Company Limited. As passenger traffic increased, extra cars were built locally to increase the number of cars in service. The first double-deck trams went into service in 1912. The company name changed to Hong Kong Tramways Limited on May 26, 1922. Six new totally enclosed double-deck cars went into service in 1925 bringing the fleet size to eighty-six. In 1929, 27 million passengers were carried, the Shaukiwan turning circle was installed in 1929, sections of the line were doubled tracked, and only one mile of single track remained.

On December 7, 1941, the Japanese attacked Hong Kong, damaging overhead wire and track, but repairs were made and service resumed. Hong Kong surrendered on December 25, 1941. Initially service resumed with about twelve cars between Causeway Bay and Western Market, because this was the only undamaged track section. In November 1944, tram service ended, because there was insufficient power available for the trams. After Hong Kong was re-occupied by British troops in August 1945, the full fleet of 109 cars still existed, but only fifteen trams were useable. The British Royal Navy arrived to get the tram electric supply back in operation plus helped in overhauling trams. In October 1945, tram service restarted with forty cars.

Questions were raised about operating trams in Hong Kong after the war. In 1946, S. R. Geary, vice president of the UK Institute of Transport and formerly of London Transport, was invited to inspect the system and make recommendations. He recommended keeping the trams, noting, "the short haul, highly peaked traffic, the ability of the tramway cars to carry excessive loads, good maintenance in all departments, and the very considerable value and long remaining life of existing assets, I do not recommend any change from tramway operations for many years to come." He commented, "The track is in exceptionally good order and compares favorably with any tramway I have seen in the United Kingdom, the U.S.A., or Canada."

By March 1947, tram services were restored to 1941 timetables. In 1948, a new tram car was designed and completed in 1949. With a fleet of 127 cars in 1955, there were 121 trams in service leaving little room for breakdowns. By 1956, there were 146 trams in the fleet. In 1964, three double-deck trams (Nos. 160–162) arrived built by the Taikoo Dockyard & Engineering Company. During 1989, two new depots, Whitty Street Depot (West Depot) and Sai Wan Ho Depot (East Depot), were built replacing the Sharp Street Depot that was redeveloped into a modern office/shopping complex. In 2014, Hong Kong trams marked 110 years of service.

In 2009, a 50 percent stake and operating rights were obtained by Veolia Transport RATP (now RATP Dev Transdev Asia) followed by full ownership in 2010. In 2014, there were 165 double-axle, double-decker trams. The trams have sliding windows. Daily ridership was 131,000 in 2021.

The Hong Kong tram map shows the system in 1979. In 2022, tram routings are: 1: Western Market–Shau Kei Wan; 2: Happy Valley–Shau Kei Wan; 3: Shek Tong Tsui–North Point; 4: Shek Tong Tsui–Causeway Bay; 5: Kennedy Town–Happy Valley; 6: Kennedy Town–Shau Kei Wan.

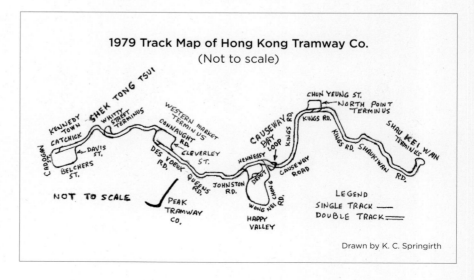

1979 Track Map of Hong Kong Tramway Co.
(Not to scale)

Drawn by K. C. Springirth

Hong Kong Tramways has a special driver training tram for operator instruction in this July 5, 1979 scene. Hong Kong's congested streets make tram driving a challenge. The year 2022 marks the 118th anniversary of Hong Kong's tram operation which started in 1904. (*Kenneth C. Springirth photograph*)

On July 5, 1979, white-painted Hong Kong Tramways' double-deck tram No. 1 with its all over advertising is alongside a double-deck bus in downtown Hong Kong. This car was built by Taikoo Dockyard and Engineering Company and placed in service on January 29, 1954. Hong Kong Tramways has the largest fleet of double-deck trams in the world. (*Kenneth C. Springirth photograph*)

Tram No. 3 (built by Taikoo Dockyard and Engineering Company and placed in service on March 31, 1952) with a tram and double-deck bus behind it are making their way on a crowded Hong Kong street on July 5, 1979. (*Kenneth C. Springirth photograph*)

Advertising a United States fast food restaurant on July 5, 1979, Hong Kong tram No. 12 (built by Hong Kong Tramways Limited and placed in service on August 23, 1952) is followed by tram No. 142 (built by Taikoo Dockyard & Engineering Company that was placed in service on March 13, 1956). (*Kenneth C. Springirth photograph*)

Passing by a tram stop on July 5, 1979 is an eye-catching orange and black "Crocodile" fashion advertisement on tram car No. 17 (built by Taikoo Dockyard & Engineering Company and was placed in service on November 9, 1953). Almost all of the trams have full body advertisements. (*Kenneth C. Springirth photograph*)

Advertising Olympus cameras is tram car No. 18 built by Taikoo Dockyard & Engineering Company and placed in service on December 11, 1952. In this July 5, 1979 scene, Hong Kong trams fit perfectly in the hustle and bustle of the city. (*Kenneth C. Springirth photograph*)

On July 5, 1979, a brilliant advertisement for Top Gear Furniture neatly appears on tram No. 47 (built by Taikoo Dockyard & Engineering Company and placed in service on December 24, 1951) and behind it tram No. 56 (built by Hong Kong & Whampoa [Kowloon] Docks) and placed in service on April 5, 1951. (*Kenneth C. Springirth photograph*)

On July 5, 1979, almost every Hong Kong tram, even those in the regular HK Tram Green, has many advertisements as evidenced by tram No. 63 (built by Taikoo Dockyard & Engineering Company and placed in service on February 28, 1953) passing tram No. 134 (built by Taikoo Dockyard & Engineering Company and placed in service on September 13, 1955). (*Kenneth C. Springirth photograph*)

On July 5, 1979, watches and cigarettes are the advertisements on the front of tram No. 68 (built by Taikoo Dockyard & Engineering Company and placed in service on May 28, 1952). (*Kenneth C. Springirth photograph*)

In this July 5, 1979 scene, a rainbow of colors typifies Kodak with their cameras and film showing well on tram No. 80 (built by Hongkong & Whampoa [Kowloon] Docks and placed in service on June 11, 1951). (*Kenneth C. Springirth photograph*)

On July 5, 1979, for people who are crazy about their food, tram No. 89 in a silver paint scheme focuses on nuts. This tram was built by Taikoo Dockyard & Engineering Company and placed in service on September 27, 1952. (*Kenneth C. Springirth photograph*)

From left to right in this July 5, 1979 scene, Northwest Orient Airlines proudly points to its daily flights to New York on tram No. 99 (built by Taikoo Dockyard & Engineering Company and placed in service on February 8, 1955) which is following tram No. 25 (built by Hongkong & Whampoa Docks and placed in service on February 27, 1952). (*Kenneth C. Springirth photograph*)

This July 5, 1979 scene shows tram No. 112 (built by Taikoo Dockyard & Engineering Company and placed in service on February 8, 1955) is passing tram No. 48 (built by Taikoo Dockyard & Engineering Company and placed in service on June 26, 1951) which is being followed by tram No. 158 (built by Taikoo Dockyard & Engineering Company and placed in service on December 12, 1963). (*Kenneth C. Springirth photograph*)

On July 5, 1979, "Fly KLM 747 fastest direct Amsterdam" is the very attention getting advertisement on tram No.113 (built by Taikoo Dockyard & Engineering Company and placed in service on May 29, 1955). (*Kenneth C. Springirth photograph*)

"Catch our Spirit to Canada" is the CP Air advertisement on tram No. 144 (built by Taikoo Dockyard & Engineering Company and placed in service on April 14, 1956) in this sunny July 5, 1979 scene. (*Kenneth C. Springirth photograph*)

On July 5, 1979, Belgian Bank has a stunning yellow advertisement on tram No. 154 (built by Hong Kong Tramways Limited and placed in service on March 2, 1962). (*Kenneth C. Springirth photograph*)

Trams can bunch up such as this July 5, 1979 scene with tram No. 155 (built by Hong Kong Tramways Limited and placed in service on April 16, 1962), followed by tram No. 68 (built by Taikoo Dockyard & Engineering Company and placed in service on May 28, 1952), followed by tram No. 74 (built by Taikoo Dockyard & Engineering Company and placed in service on March 26, 1951), and followed by additional trams. (*Kenneth C. Springirth photograph*)

On July 5, 1979, tram No. 160 (built by Taikoo Dockyard & Engineering Company and placed in service on January 21, 1964) is pulling trailer No. 11 (built by Metal Sections Ltd. of Oldbury, England with assembly on trucks made by the Taiko Dockyard) was placed in service on March 10, 1966. With increasing numbers of passengers, the first single-deck trailer No. 1 was placed in service on August 6, 1964, and by September 23, 1967 there were twenty-two trailers in service. They were withdrawn from service in 1982 due to frequent derailments and being uneconomical to run because each trailer required a separate conductor. (*Kenneth C. Springirth photograph*)